rhetoric

EDITED BY
richard l. larson
UNIVERSITY OF HAWAII

THE BOBBS-MERRILL COMPANY, INC.
A SUBSIDIARY OF HOWARD W. SAMS AND CO., INC.
INDIANAPOLIS   NEW YORK

THE BOBBS-MERRILL SERIES IN COMPOSITION AND RHETORIC

General Editors:

FALK S. JOHNSON   JAMES R. KREUZER   FRANKLIN NORVISH

Richard L. Larson is associate professor of English and director of composition at the University of Hawaii. He received his A.B., A.M., and Ph.D. at Harvard University. Mr. Larson has contributed many articles to scholarly journals and is the author of A RHETORICAL GUIDE TO THE BORZOI COLLEGE READER *(1967).*

COPYRIGHT © 1968 BY THE BOBBS-MERRILL COMPANY, INC.
PRINTED IN THE UNITED STATES OF AMERICA
Library of Congress Catalog Card Number 67-23042
FIRST PRINTING

contents

introduction

TODAY when someone applies the term "rhetoric" to a written or oral discourse, he is likely to be expressing at least mild disapproval. He may mean that the discourse is inflated or bombastic, full of gaudy metaphors and loosely connotative words, or that it tries to arouse feelings out of proportion to those warranted by the subject, or that it is deceptive, even fraudulent. A teacher, observing the emotional language in a student's writing, may reprimand him for "melodramatic rhetoric," meaning that he has used purposelessly elevated or figurative language. An educated reader may call an advertisement sheer "rhetoric," and mean that the advertised product can hardly be expected to accomplish all that is claimed for it. Newspapermen commenting on a speech by a federal official may—and sometimes do—dismiss the speaker's words as just more of the "rhetoric of the Great Society," and mean that the speaker is restating platitudes or repeating promises that can never be kept.

Why, then, compile a group of readings for university students around a term whose connotations are so unfavorable? The answer, simply, is that the term "rhetoric" has not always had the negative implications just mentioned, nor is it used with these implications by many university teachers of English and speech. Although in current popular usage "rhetoric" names a characteristic (usually not admirable) of speech and writing or expresses an evaluation of the reliability of a discourse, historically it did not refer to what the speaker said or the writer wrote. It referred to the principles that guide effective speaking and writing. "Rhetoric," to give one definition here briefly, was the name given to the art of speaking (and writing) effectively. To elaborate the definition in language not unfair to most users of the term in earlier centuries, it was in any discourse—spoken or written—the art of selecting some matter for presentation, a plan of organization, and a style that were (all three) appropriate to the audience, purpose, and occasion for speaking or writing.

The principles and value of this art called "rhetoric" have interested some of the most eminent Western thinkers since before the time of Plato (including religious philosophers such as St. Augustine). To be sure, little was added to our knowledge about the art during the two or three centuries preceding our own. Some Renaissance and later theorists restricted the meaning of "rhetoric" to "the technique of stylistic embellishment." Some eighteenth-century theorists sought to embrace under "rhetoric" studies of the workings of metaphor and of the emotional effects of various kinds of discourse, including imaginative literature. Most of these studies were unproductive but, despite the failure of viable new theories to emerge, "rhetoric" (defined as the study of how to write and speak well) remained a staple of the curriculum in many English (and some American) schools. It is still taught, or at least the name is used to designate courses in writing and speaking in many schools and universities. Since 1930, "rhetoric," defined as a study of the art and even more of the process of communication, has been attracting so much attention among scholars—of literature and language, and of psychology, sociology, and anthropology—that a "revival of rhetoric" is said to be in progress.

This "revival" is not simply a renewal of interest in rhetorical theories of the past, although scholars are reevaluating these theories. The "revival" is also a refreshment, even a redirection, of rhetorical studies. Rhetoric is coming to be regarded as an aid in the making of public decisions—not just a method of inducing readers to believe in decisions already made. As part of the study of rhetoric, scholars are analyzing the techniques of expression used by important modern writers and attempting to determine what causes a discourse to have its special effect on a reader. In discussing the art of rhetoric, some teachers are asking students to analyze for themselves the probable effects on their hearers of different ways of expressing a particular idea. They are telling their students to use the results of these analyses in choosing the most effective way of expressing that idea. Rhetoric is itself becoming an art of decision-making.

The major purpose of this collection is to introduce students to several writers who are part of the illustrious tradition of rhetorical study and to sample the recent developments in rhetorical theory that are continuing even as we study these selections. A second, but by no means unimportant, purpose in presenting these excerpts is to enable students to consider whether the teachings of these leading theorists might be of value in their own writing and speaking.

Although most theorists of rhetoric unfold the art of effective communication, or, in the hope of improving the art, inquire into the processes of communication, or do both, they naturally differ in the questions they emphasize and the paths they take toward understanding the art. These differences of approach and emphasis are the bases for grouping the selections. (Some writers who treat the entire subject of rhetoric must appear in more than one group.) This grouping, it is to be hoped, will bring into focus the major preoccupations of both classical and modern writers, while enabling the reader to compare the methods of inquiry used by different writers in addressing similar problems in rhetoric.

The selections in Part I address the problem of definition: What is "rhetoric"? The problem is more complicated than our first paragraphs implied, since the referent of the term, not to mention its scope, is hardly settled. Is rhetoric *1* a body of theory about communication, *2* a quality that some discourse has (and other discourse does not have), *3* the name given to a piece (or collection of pieces) of persuasive discourse, *4* the name given to those techniques or devices (taken as a group) used by a writer to influence an audience, *5* the name given to a body of rules for writing well, or *6* the art of making wise decisions about discourse (see ¶ 4, p. 5)? If, as some classical theorists held, rhetoric is the art of effective communication as taught by "rhetoricians," what is the character of that art? What is its purpose? And what is its value?

Plato, addressing questions about the character and value of what rhetoricians teach, gave two seemingly contradictory answers at different periods in his life. His first answer (mentioned in the headnote and questions on the first selection) is similar to the current popular conceptions of "rhetoric" mentioned earlier; his second suggests an honorable and intellectually honest standard for the student of rhetoric to seek. Aristotle characterizes the art called rhetoric without judging that art either as comprehensively or as idealistically as Plato does, although Aristotle implies that knowledge of the art can benefit the speaker and his society. Cicero insists that rhetoric is important for the public servant, though he does not go as far as Quintilian does (in a selection not included here) when the latter builds the assumption of the orator's

moral excellence into his definition of rhetoric and erects his entire theory on that assumption. Kenneth Burke and Donald Bryant, like many twentieth-century theorists, considerably widen the reference of the term "rhetoric." In Burke's definition the findings of anthropologists, sociologists, and psychologists bear on the study of rhetoric as much as the findings of linguists and literary scholars, for all are studying activities in which a speaker or performer wishes his audience to "identify" with him. Bryant does not extend the definition of the term as far as Burke, but the kinds of discourse he can call "rhetorical" and the values he thinks such discourse can have in our society go far beyond anything that Plato, Aristotle, and Cicero imply. In the last selection in Part I, Martin Steinmann, Jr., narrows the scope of the term "rhetoric" in order to facilitate more precise and fruitful research into how a writer or speaker makes his effects.

Most of the selections in Part II are from the pedagogy of rhetoric. Assuming that there is value to an art of communicating effectively, the authors offer advice to students on finding material and arranging it. Aristotle's catalog of "topics," or ways of thinking that might suggest arguments, is a survey rather than a textbook, but he implied that the first step in teaching rhetoric was to make the student aware of possible techniques for invention. Cicero, too, summarizes well-known doctrines about the structure of an oration in such a way that students of rhetoric can follow these doctrines. The works of Quintilian and Whately were intended and used as textbooks; although both offer advice about locating arguments, Whately's interest was more in selecting, arranging, and proportioning arguments already located. Martin and Ohmann attempt to guide students in the appropriate use of particular logical and rhetorical techniques. Robert Gorrell suggests a new principle to guide invention and organization. Gorrell asserts that the writer (when he begins writing) enters into an agreement with his reader to accomplish particular acts, and, thus, the writer's task is to keep his agreement and not just to achieve an effect.

In Part III the differences in the interests of classical and modern theorists are much clearer than in Part I and Part II. Quintilian regards language as only one feature of discourse, to be studied (parallel to the selection and arrangement of material) under the abstract heading of "elocutio," or, loosely, "expression." Quintilian's doctrine of stylistic "decorum" (an admonition to use only words and idioms that fit the occasion) is reflected in many early eighteenth-century writings on style; his identification of three styles again reveals the classical rhetorician's effort to generalize, organize, and classify the precepts of the art.

Many twentieth-century rhetoricians, however, have refused to repeat the easy (and general) admonitions about style that earlier rhetoricians accepted. I. A. Richards, in particular, insists that the study of rhetoric must begin with the study of language, and he redefines the term "rhetoric" as the study of how words work and how meanings are understood. For Francis Christensen, one of the most influential teachers of the rhetoric of written English in this decade, the study of rhetoric begins with the building of sentences and continues with the building of paragraphs—a sequence not found in any of the classical rhetoricians who divided their works into sections on Invention, Disposition, Elocution, Memory, and Delivery. Josephine Miles seeks in the study of grammar a way of talking about the choices open to the writer as he composes a sentence, and in the process she arrives at a way of describing prose style. If there is to be a "modern" rhetoric, it may begin in studies of semantics and grammar such as those on which the works of Richards, Christensen, and Miles are founded.

A collection of works on classical and modern rhetoric might well include illustrations of the practice of rhetoric, but space permits only the naming of several writers whose works might furnish such illustrations. Swift, Burke, *The Federalist Papers,* Lincoln, and—from our own day—George Orwell, James Baldwin, Aldous Huxley, Martin Luther King, Adlai Stevenson, and John Kennedy, to name just a few, will repay study by any readers who, overwhelmed by the diversity of rhetorical theories represented here, wish to see those theories confirmed or disproved in practice by speakers and writers.

Such a desire to test these theories, in fact, would be the best attitude that could come from the study of this collection. Are the theories and doctrines of classical rhetoric helpful to an understanding of how discourse works? Are the theories of modern rhetoricians any more helpful? What do these rhetoricians value in writing? What views of language underlie their theories? Are these theories useful as guides for today's speakers and writers? Does the new interest in grammar and semantics among twentieth-century scholars promise to shed more light on the workings of spoken and written discourse than older theorists' attention to finding and arranging materials has done? Which of the descriptions of grammar available today has most promise for this purpose? What assumptions do classical and modern rhetoricians make about human beings and the way they respond to communication, and how good are these assumptions? How, fundamentally, does spoken and written discourse make its effect, and can the process be described in words? What tests, what analyses, do we need to make in order to refine a theory of rhetoric to the point where it will be truly useful in the study and teaching of discourse?

In facing these questions, the student will be participating, as all students of rhetoric must, in the process of inquiry by which our understanding of the creation and functioning of written and oral discourse is advanced.

RICHARD L. LARSON

bibliography

Bailey, Dudley. *Essays on Rhetoric*. New York, 1965.

——. "A Plea for a Modern Set of Topoi," *College English*, XXVI, No. 2 (November 1964), 111–117.

Baldwin, Charles S. *Ancient Rhetoric and Poetic*. New York, 1924.

——. *Medieval Rhetoric to 1400*. New York, 1928.

Booth, Wayne C. *The Rhetoric of Fiction*. Chicago, 1961.

——. "The Rhetorical Stance," *College Composition and Communication*, XIV, No. 3 (October 1963), 139–145.

Braddock, Richard. "Crucial Issues," *College Composition and Communication*, XVI, No. 3 (October 1965), 165–169.

Brown, Huntington. *Prose Styles: Five Primary Types*. Minneapolis, Minnesota, 1966.

Christensen, Francis. "A Generative Rhetoric of the Paragraph," *College Composition and Communication*, XVI, No. 3 (October 1965), 144–156.

——. *Notes toward a New Rhetoric*. New York, 1967.

Christensen, Francis, *et al*. *The Sentence and the Paragraph*. Champaign, Illinois, 1966.

Corbett, Edward P. J. *Classical Rhetoric for the Modern Student*. New York, 1965.

Croll, Morris W. *Style, Rhetoric, and Rhythm*. Princeton, New Jersey, 1966.

Gibson, Walker. *Tough, Sweet, and Stuffy: An Essay on Modern American Prose Styles*. Bloomington, Indiana, 1966.

Hunt, Everett L. "Plato and Aristotle on Rhetoric and Rhetoricians," in L. G. Crocker and P. A. Carmack, *Readings in Rhetoric*. Springfield, Illinois, 1965. Pp. 100–159.

Joos, Martin. *The Five Clocks*. Bloomington, Indiana, 1962. An essay, by a linguist, on different kinds of style.

Larson, Richard L. "Sentences in Action: A Technique for Analyzing Paragraphs," *College Composition and Communication*, XVIII, No. 1 (February 1967), 16–22.

Natanson, Maurice, and Henry W. Johnstone, Jr. *Philosophy, Rhetoric, and Argumentation*. University Park, Pennsylvania, 1965.

Ohmann, Richard M. "Literature as Sentences," *College English*, XXVII, No. 4 (January 1966), 261–267.

——. *Shaw: The Style and the Man*. Middletown, Connecticut, 1962. Another important essay by Professor Ohmann appears in Steinmann, *New Rhetorics*, listed below.

Parker, John. "Some Organizational Variables and Their Effect upon Comprehension," *Journal of Communication*, XII (March 2, 1962), 27–32.

Schwartz, Joseph, and John Rycenga. *The Province of Rhetoric*. New York, 1965.

Sledd, James. "Some Notes on English Prose Style," in *A Short Introduction to English Grammar*. Chicago, 1959. Pp. 259–334.

Steinmann, Martin, Jr., ed. *New Rhetorics*. New York, 1967. An important collection of essays.

Swiggart, Peter. *Anatomy of Writing*. New York, 1966.

Ulanov, Barry. "The Relevance of Rhetoric," in *Rhetoric and School Programs*. Champaign, Illinois, 1966. Pp. 1–6.

Weaver, Richard. *The Ethics of Rhetoric*. Chicago, 1957.

Wilson, John. *Thinking with Concepts*. Cambridge, England, 1963.

In the Athens of the fourth century B.C., skill in oratory was considered essential for any citizen who hoped to succeed in public life, and most citizens were expected to take part in politics. Skill in oratory was frequently important to the citizen's private affairs as well, especially if he engaged (as many citizens did) in litigations before courts composed of his fellow citizens. As a result, teachers of oratory (among them a group called the Sophists) earned popularity and prosperity from helping citizens learn to speak well.

The duties and responsibilities of the orator are prominent subjects of discussion in two of Plato's dialogues: the GORGIAS and the PHAEDRUS. In GORGIAS (which is thought to be one of Plato's earlier dialogues), Socrates, who died in 399 B.C., reveals his distrust of rhetoricians, or teachers of oratory; they teach speakers how to make ideas appear convincing, he contends, rather than helping them to engage in a search for truth and justice. In PHAEDRUS, evidently written some fifteen years after GORGIAS, Socrates discusses rhetoric more extensively and more subtly than in the earlier dialogue. PHAEDRUS is often read as proof that Plato had changed his opinion of rhetoric, even though Socrates again censures the superficiality in much contemporary teaching of rhetoric. The apparent differences in attitude between the two dialogues may be only the result of different emphases. In GORGIAS Socrates is evaluating contemporary practice in the teaching of oratory (or rhetoric), whereas in PHAEDRUS he is telling what an art of rhetoric ought to be if it is to deserve approval.

PHAEDRUS (from which the selection below is taken) begins with three formal speeches on the subject of love, which serve as points of departure and illustrations for a comparison of good and bad rhetoric. Phaedrus himself is characterized only as a friend of Socrates whose views, at the start, are closer to those of the Sophists than to those of Socrates.

the ideal orator

PLATO

SOCRATES. Well then, take the subject we were just now proposing to examine, how a discourse should be formed in order to be written well, or the reverse. This matter ought to be looked into.

PHAEDRUS. Surely.

SOCRATES. Come, now. What is needed in advance if an utterance is to be good and fine? Must not the mind of the one who utters it be cognizant of the truth about the matters he is going to discuss?

PHAEDRUS. And yet, friend Socrates, on that point I have heard differently. I have heard that one who plans to be an orator lies under no necessity of learning what is actually right, but must learn what seems right to the crowd who are to pass judgment,

FROM PLATO, *Phaedrus, Ion, Gorgias, and Symposium, with Passages from the Republic and Laws,* TRANS. LANE COOPER (NEW YORK: OXFORD UNIVERSITY PRESS, 1948), PP. 45–48, 60–69. COPYRIGHT 1938 BY LANE COOPER. USED BY PERMISSION OF CORNELL UNIVERSITY PRESS.

nor yet what is really good and beautiful, but what is going to seem so. From these appearances, they say, comes persuasion, and not from the truth.

SOCRATES. What "they say," Phaedrus, "must not be cast aside," if they who say it are indeed wise, but must be examined on the chance that there may be something in it; so we must not hastily dismiss this statement now.

PHAEDRUS. Quite right.

SOCRATES. Let us examine it in this way. . . .

PHAEDRUS. How?

SOCRATES. Well, suppose I were trying to persuade you to secure a horse and go against the enemy, and neither of us knew what a horse was like, but I happened to know so much about you, namely, that Phaedrus thinks a horse to be that one of the domestic animals which has the longest ears. . . .

PHAEDRUS. That, Socrates, would be ridiculous!

SOCRATES. Wait! Suppose I were in sober earnest trying to persuade you with a speech I had composed in honor of an ass, which I called a horse, where I said he was invaluable as a beast to own at home and on campaign—you could use him as a mount in battle, he would serve to carry baggage, he would be helpful in a great variety of ways. . . .

PHAEDRUS. The whole thing would be utterly absurd.

SOCRATES. Yes, but isn't absurdity in a friend better than crafty speaking in a foe?

PHAEDRUS. It would seem so.

SOCRATES. Well then, take the artful rhetorician who does not know what good and evil are, and essays to persuade an equally ignorant State, not by an encomium on "the shadow of an ass," instead of "horse," but by recommending evil as if it were good. When, having studied the opinions of the crowd, he persuades them to do evil deeds instead of good, what sort of harvest, think you, will the art of rhetoric thereafter reap from the seed it has sown?

PHAEDRUS. No welcome harvest, surely.

SOCRATES. Come now, good friend. Haven't we been too harsh in condemnation of the Art of making speeches? She might well say: "Strange creatures, why do you talk such nonsense? I never force a man to take up speaking when he is ignorant of the truth, but, if you grant that my advice has any value, he will acquire the knowledge first, then come to me. The one great point I make is this, that, without me, the man who knows the actual truth of things is not thereby a whit the nearer to a mastery of persuasion."

PHAEDRUS. And will she not be right in saying that?

SOCRATES. I grant you, yes—if the arguments that come to her trial bear witness that she is an art; for I seem as it were to hear some arguments approaching and protesting that she lies, and that Rhetoric is no art, but a trade devoid of art. "A solid art of speaking," says the Spartan, "without a grip on truth, there is not nor will be hereafter, ever."

PHAEDRUS. These arguments, Socrates, we need them! Bring on the witnesses, and examine them for the matter and the manner of their telling!

SOCRATES. Come hither, noble creatures, and persuade our Phaedrus, sire of lovely offspring, that unless he has paid due attention to philosophy, he never will be competent to speak on any subject. And let Phaedrus answer.

PHAEDRUS. Ask on!

SOCRATES. Now then. Taken as a whole, is not Rhetoric the art of winning the soul by discourse, which means not merely argument in the courts of justice, and all other sorts of public councils, but in private conference as well? Is it not one thing, and the same, whether it has to do with matters great or small; always intrinsically honorable—I mean, of course, *right* Rhetoric—whether the points at issue are serious or not? Is that approximately what you have heard? . . .

[Socrates and Phaedrus analyze the previous speeches and point out the inadequacies in contemporary rhetorical theory. Socrates introduces the concept of dialectic—the systematic analysis and combination of species—as the process leading to true knowledge.]

SOCRATES. . . . But I am willing to tell how one should write if the result is to be as artistic as it may be.

PHAEDRUS. Tell on.

SOCRATES. The function of a speech, we saw, is to win the soul; and hence the man who aims to be an artistic speaker must necessarily know the soul in all its species. There are so and so many kinds of souls, of such and such a nature, and hence men severally are of such a sort, and such another. Once these distinctions have been made, we come, in turn, to speeches [arguments]: there are so and so many kinds of them, each kind of such or such a nature. Now then, men of a given sort under speeches of a given nature, and through that cause, are readily brought to such and such convictions; whereas men of another given sort are made incredulous through this and this. When one has these matters well in mind, the next thing needed is to see them as they are in practice, and as they are effected there; a man must have the power to follow up the scent acutely. Otherwise he never will know anything more than what he heard when he attended lectures. But when he is in a competent state to say what sort of man will be persuaded by arguments of given kinds, let us suppose that he has his man at hand, can feel him out, and can tell himself with certainty: "This is the man, and this the nature, that those lectures deal with. Now the case is actually before me where I must apply just these arguments, thus, in order to effect persuasion in these definite points." Suppose that the speaker now can do all this; can add to it a grasp of the proper times for speaking and refraining; can discern, again, with regard to "Style Concise," "Style Pitiful," "Style Terrible," and all the other forms of discourse he has learned, the opportune moments, and inopportune, for using each of them. Then, and not till then, will the art be finished, be beautiful and complete. Nay more, if any one omits a single step, as speaker, or as teacher, or as writer, and avers that he writes with art, the man who disbelieves him wins. "Well then, Socrates and Phaedrus," the man who compiles a Rhetoric will say, "is this the proper view? Or should one entertain some other concept of the art of speaking?"

PHAEDRUS. I think no other view is possible, Socrates: and yet the labor involved would seem to be no trifling matter.

SOCRATES. That is true. And on that account we ought to turn all the explanations inside out, and see if there appears some other, perchance easier and shorter, way to the art, so as not to wander in vain on a long and rugged road when we have a short and smooth one. No, if you have any help to offer, something you have heard from Lysias or any other, try to recollect and tell it.

PHAEDRUS. If all depended on the trying, I might have it, but at the moment I have nothing at all to offer.

SOCRATES. Well then, would you like me to give an explanation, one that I heard from some of those who treat the subject?

PHAEDRUS. Yes, do.

SOCRATES. You know there is a saying, Phaedrus: "Even the wolf has a right to be heard."

PHAEDRUS. You be his advocate.

SOCRATES. Well, they say there is no call to be so solemn in this matter, or to go far afield with the aim of reducing all to principle, because (as we said at the opening of this discussion) a man who is going to be competent as a speaker need not possess the truth at all in questions of justice or of goodness with respect to actions, or indeed to men, so long as men are what they are by nature or through education. In the courts, they say, the truth about such questions is of absolutely no concern to any one; the thing that counts there is what will be believed, and that is "probability." To this the man who is going to speak "with art" must devote himself. What actually took place must sometimes not be mentioned even, if the way in which it happened was not "probable"; rather, it is the "probabilities" that must be adduced, alike in prosecution and in defence. In fact, under all conditions the thing to be kept in view is "probability," while the speaker often and often says good-bye to the truth. This "probability," they hold, if it be kept up steadily throughout the speech supplies the entire art of rhetoric.

PHAEDRUS. Precisely, Socrates. You have given the matter as they state it who profess to be experts in the technique of speaking. I recollect that we briefly touched upon the like in what was said before. This matter would seem to be something of extreme importance to the experts.

SOCRATES. Take Tisias now; you have studied and restudied him with care. Accordingly, let Tisias pronounce upon this question, whether by "the probable" he means aught else than what the crowd believe.

PHAEDRUS. He means just that.

SOCRATES. And it seems he has thought out the following case, at once a deep discovery and artistic secret, thus recorded: If a feeble and courageous man has beaten up a strong and cowardly one, and robbed him of his mantle or the like, and is brought to trial for it, then neither one of them must tell the truth. Instead, the coward must declare that he was not assaulted by a single man, to wit the brave one, who will counter with the statement that the two of them were alone, and will in turn advance the argument: "How could a fellow such as I lay hands on one like him?" The coward, now, will not admit his cowardice, but will try to invent some other lie, and thus no doubt give his antagonist the opening to refute him. And so for other cases, the means to artful speaking are pretty much like these. Isn't it so, my Phaedrus?

PHAEDRUS. It is.

SOCRATES. Ah, what a genius he must have been to bring to light a deeply-hidden art, this Tisias, or whoever did invent it, and whichever was the land whence he rejoices to derive his name! And yet, my friend, what shall we do? Shall we say to him, or shall we not?—

PHAEDRUS. Say what?

SOCRATES. Say this: "For some time, Tisias, indeed before you came along, we have been arguing that this 'probability' was, in fact, engendered in the masses because of its resemblance to the truth. As for resemblances, we just now stated that the man who, everywhere, best understands how to discover them is the man who knows the truth. Accordingly, if you have anything else to say about the art of speaking, we should like to hear it. If not, then we shall put our trust in the positions we recently examined. We say: Unless a man has taken to account the different natures of those who are to hear him, and unless he can divide realities according to their species, and can also comprehend particulars, taken singly, under one idea, he never will be an expert in the art of eloquence to the measure which a human being can attain. But this result never will be gained without much diligence. And by a man of wisdom the toil must be endured, not for the sake of eloquence and action before men, but in order to be able to utter what is pleasing to the gods, and in everything, with all one's power, to act in the way that will please them. No, Tisias, you see just how it is; it is just as wiser men than we are say. It is not one's fellow servants that one should care to please, if one has sense, save incidentally, but one's good and noble masters. And therefore, if the way around is long, do not marvel; for, when the ends are great, the circuit must be trod; the path is not as you conceive it. Yet your ends also, as the argument sets forth, will be best attained in this way, if they are what a man desires."

PHAEDRUS. Most admirably spoken, Socrates, it seems to me, if only one could do it.

SOCRATES. But when you strive for noble ends, it is also noble to endure whatever pain the effort may involve.

PHAEDRUS. Indeed it is.

SOCRATES. So there, on art and lack of art with reference to speaking, let that suffice.

PHAEDRUS. So be it. . . .

[In the intervening passage, Socrates explains his conviction that spoken discourse, vividly delivered, is more valuable than written discourse.]

SOCRATES. . . . Now it seems to me the question about what has art and what has not has been made fairly clear.

PHAEDRUS. Yes, it seemed so. Go back, however, and remind me how.

SOCRATES. In advance, a man must know the truth about each particular of which he speaks or writes. He must be able to define each one of them in itself. When he has defined them, he must, in turn, know how to subdivide them severally according to their species, to the point where a division cannot be carried further. By the same method of analysis he must investigate the nature of the soul, and must discover what kind of argument is adapted to each nature. This done, he must settle and order his discourse accordingly, addressing to the many-sided soul a varied speech that touches every chord, a simple one to the simple. Not till then can discourses be artistic as far as it lies in the nature of their genus to be made so, to be controlled by art for the purpose of instruction or persuasion. That is what the whole preceding argument has revealed to us.

PHAEDRUS. Most certainly it was in substance thus that the matter did come out.

SOCRATES. But what about the question whether it is fine or base to utter speeches, and to write them, and under what conditions doing so might in justice be called a disgrace or not? Was that made clear when it was said a little while ago. . . ?

PHAEDRUS. What?

SOCRATES. That if Lysias or any one else ever wrote, or shall hereafter write, in private life or in public as a statesman, any document of a political description, and imagines it has in it certainty and clearness in a high degree, then that is a disgrace to the writer, whether anybody says it is or not. Verily, awake or dreaming, to be ignorant of what is right and what is wrong, of what is good and what is bad, cannot escape from being blameful, not even if the entire mob were to applaud it.

PHAEDRUS. No indeed.

SOCRATES. But take the man who judges that in the written word, no matter what the subject, there necessarily is much that is for play; the man who thinks that no discourse, in metre or without it, is ever worth great effort in writing, or in reciting as the rhapsodes do (when all is uttered, not after critical examination, nor for instruction, but just to be believed); the man who, rather, thinks that the best things of this kind really constitute a means of recollection for those who know, while in discourses for instruction, uttered for the sake of learning, words really graven in the soul concerning justice, beauty, goodness, in these alone are clarity, perfection, and value worth the effort; the man who thinks that such discourses only should be called his children, legitimate sons as it were, first among them the word that may be found indwelling in himself, and then its off-spring, who are its brothers also, when such are by desert implanted in other souls of other men; the man who lets all other discourses go their way rejoicing. That man, perchance, my Phaedrus, is such a one as you and I would pray we both of us might become. . . .

suggestions for discussion and writing

1. What, according to Socrates, are the essential qualifications of the "good" orator? What does Socrates say about the moral character of the ideal speaker? What is the importance of these comments for Socrates' theory of rhetoric? Have these comments any importance in relation to problems in the practice of rhetoric today?

2. In *Gorgias,* Socrates had labeled oratory (rhetoric) a species of pandering, one subdivision of which is cookery—"an occupation which masquerades as an art but in my opinion is no more than a knack acquired by routine." A few sentences later he groups oratory and beauty-culture together, and still later adds that pandering "catches fools with the bait of ephemeral pleasure and tricks them into holding it in the highest esteem" (*Gorgias,* trans. W. A. Hamilton [Penguin Books, 1960], pp. 44, 46). In *Phaedrus,* does Socrates contradict these statements? Where? Why? If you think he does not contradict them, explain how you might reconcile the views expressed in the two dialogues.

3. What is the distinction between "probability" and "truth" that Socrates makes? Give an example of each.

4. Enumerate the parts or subdivisions of the rhetorician's art, as Socrates sees them.

5. If the rhetorician knows and is speaking the "truth," why does he need to concern himself with the workings of men's souls? In concerning himself with how to reach men's souls, is he not guilty of the same practices Socrates condemns on pp. 9–10? How would Socrates reconcile this possible contradiction?

6. After isolating the steps in the composition of a speech (or persuasive essay) enumerated by Socrates, compose an essay of your own in which you follow these steps precisely, and then evaluate the result.

Aristotle, a pupil of Plato, finished his RHETORIC *forty to fifty years after the* PHAEDRUS. *The* RHETORIC *is not a systematic treatise; it is thought to be a compilation of lecture notes used by Aristotle in his teaching of the subject. Rather than a statement of goals for an ideal rhetoric, Aristotle's* RHETORIC *is a summarization and an analysis of what is known about methods of persuading different audiences in different situations. The outstanding feature of Aristotle's* RHETORIC—*not represented in this collection because of its length—is his analysis of the various kinds of human emotions and of the means by which an orator can appeal to each. Partly because of this analysis, but also because of Aristotle's thoroughness in reviewing important features and techniques of rhetoric, the work is an important text for students of rhetoric even today. The passage that follows, from Chapter I of Book I, describes rhetoric as an art, the art of speaking, coordinate in importance with dialectic (logical analysis).*

what rhetoric is

ARISTOTLE

BUT the art of rhetoric has its value. It is valuable, first, because truth and justice are by nature more powerful than their opposites; so that, when decisions are not made as they should be, the speakers with the right on their side have only themselves to thank for the outcome. Their neglect of the art needs correction. [A proper knowledge and exercise of Rhetoric would prevent the triumph of fraud and injustice.] Secondly, [Rhetoric is valuable as a means of instruction]. Even if our speaker had the most accurate scientific information, still there are persons whom he could not readily persuade with scientific arguments. True instruction, by the method of logic, is here impossible; the speaker must frame his proofs and arguments with the help of common knowledge and accepted opinions. . . . Thirdly, in Rhetoric, as in Dialectic, we should be able to argue on either side of a question; not with a view to putting both sides into practice—we must not advocate evil—but in order that no aspect of the case may escape us, and that if our opponent makes unfair use of the arguments, we may be able in turn to refute them. In no other art do we draw opposite conclusions; it is characteristic of Rhetoric and Dialectic alone that, abstractly considered, they may indifferently prove opposite statements. Still, their basis, in the facts, is not a matter of indifference, for, speaking broadly, what is true and preferable is by nature always easier to prove, and more convincing. Lastly, if it is a disgrace to a man when he cannot defend himself

FROM *The Rhetoric of Aristotle,* TRANS. LANE COOPER (NEW YORK: APPLETON-CENTURY-CROFTS, INC., 1960), PP. 5—11. COPYRIGHT 1932, 1960 BY LANE COOPER. REPRINTED BY PERMISSION OF APPLETON-CENTURY-CROFTS. MATERIAL WITHIN BRACKETS HAS BEEN INTERPOLATED BY THE TRANSLATOR IN ORDER TO EXPLAIN OCCASIONALLY CRYPTIC PASSAGES AND REFERENCES IN THE TEXT.

in a bodily way, it would be odd not to think him disgraced when he cannot defend himself with reason [in a speech]. Reason is more distinctive of man than is bodily effort. If it is urged that an abuse of the rhetorical faculty can work great mischief, the same charge can be brought against all good things (save virtue itself), and especially against the most useful things such as strength, health, wealth, and military skill. Rightly employed, they work the greatest blessings; and wrongly employed, they work the utmost harm.

We have seen that Rhetoric is not confined to any single and definite class of subjects, but in this respect is like Dialectic, and that the art has its uses; and we see that its function is not [absolutely] to persuade, but to discover the available means of persuasion in a given case. [Not outward success, but a correct method, is the criterion of art; the correct method will bring success in proportion. An unwarranted appeal to the emotions might win an undesirable success.] Herein Rhetoric is like all other arts. Thus the aim of medicine is not, strictly speaking, to restore a sick man to perfect health, but to bring him as near to health as the case admits; people who never can be well may yet be properly treated. Further, we see that it is the office of one and the same art to discern the genuine means, and also the spurious means, of persuasion, just as it is the office of Dialectic to discern the true, and also the sham, syllogism; for sophistical dialectic, or sophistical speaking, is made so, not by the faculty, but by the moral purpose. [The faculty is the same in both arts.] There is this difference, however: we apply the term "rhetorician" alike to describe a speaker's command of the art and a speaker's moral purpose; whereas, in the field of Dialectic, the term "sophist" refers to the moral purpose, while "dialectician" applies to the faculty [the normal function].

[Having thus made clear that Rhetoric is an art, and when rightly practised an honest and useful art,] we must now proceed to discuss its method—the mode and the means that will enable us to attain to the proper ends. Accordingly, let us start afresh, as it were, first defining, and then going on to the rest.

1. 2. [DEFINITION OF RHETORIC. MODES AND MEANS OF PERSUASION.] So let Rhetoric be defined as the faculty [power] of discovering in the particular case what are the available means of persuasion. This is the function of no other art [save Dialectic].

The others are each instructive or persuasive with regard to some special subject-matter. Thus medicine informs us about the conditions of health and disease; geometry about the properties of magnitudes; arithmetic about numbers; and so with the rest of the arts and sciences. But Rhetoric, it would seem, has the function of discovering the means of persuasion for every case, so to speak, that is offered; and hence we say that the art as such has no special application to any distinct class of subjects.

Proofs [persuasions] are of two kinds, artistic and non-artistic. [Or we might call them "scientific" and "unscientific." Aristotle distinguishes means of persuasion that inherently belong *in* the art, and those that, while associated with it, are really external and adventitious.] By "non-artistic" proofs are meant all such as are not supplied by our own efforts, but existed beforehand, such as witnesses, admissions under torture, written contracts, and the like. By "artistic" proofs [means of persuasion] are meant those that may be furnished by the method of Rhetoric through our own efforts. The first sort have only to be used; the second have to be found.

Of the means of persuasion supplied by the speech itself there are three kinds. The first kind reside in the character [*ethos*] of the speaker; the second consist in producing a certain [the right] attitude in the hearer; the third appertain to the argument proper, in so far as it actually or seemingly demonstrates.

The character [*ethos*] of the speaker is a cause of persuasion when the speech is so uttered as to make him worthy of belief; for as a rule we trust men of probity more, and more quickly, about things in general, while on points outside the realm of exact knowledge, where opinion is divided, we trust them absolutely. This trust, however, should be created by the speech itself, and not left to depend upon an antecedent impression that the speaker is this or that kind of man. It is not true, as some writers on the art maintain, that the probity of the speaker contributes nothing to his persuasiveness; on the contrary, we might almost affirm that his character [*ethos*] is the most potent of all the means to persuasion.

Secondly, persuasion is effected through the audience, when they are brought by the speech into a state of emotion; for we give very different decisions under the sway of pain or joy, and liking or hatred. This, we contend, is the sole aspect of the art with which technical writers of the day have tried to deal. We shall elucidate it in detail when we come to discuss the emotions.

Thirdly, persuasion is effected by the arguments, when we demonstrate the truth, real or apparent, by such means as inhere in particular cases.

Such being the instruments of persuasion, to master all three obviously calls for a man who can reason logically, can analyze the types of human character [*ethe*], along with the virtues, and, thirdly, can analyze the emotions—the nature and quality of each several emotion, with the means by which, and the manner in which, it is excited. Thus it follows that Rhetoric is a kind of offshoot, on the one hand, of Dialectic, and on the other, of that study of Ethics which may properly be called "political." [With Aristotle, Ethics, the science dealing with individual conduct, shades off into Politics (a border subject), which deals with the conduct and activities of men in groups—of the State.] And hence it is that Rhetoric, and those who profess it, slip into the guise of Politics [and political experts], whether from defects of education, or through quackery [imposture], or from other human failings. As we said at the outset, Rhetoric is a branch of Dialectic, and resembles that. Neither of them is a *science*, with a definite subject-matter; both are *faculties* for providing arguments. On their function, and on their relation to each other, perhaps enough has now been said.

[Let us turn to the instruments of persuasion.] As for real or apparent demonstration, there are in Rhetoric two modes, corresponding to the two modes in Dialectic. As in Dialectic we have, on the one hand, induction, and, on the other, the syllogism and apparent syllogism, so in Rhetoric: the example is a form of induction; while the enthymeme is a syllogism, and the apparent enthymeme an apparent syllogism. "Enthymeme" is the name I give to a rhetorical syllogism, "example" to a rhetorical induction. Whenever men in speaking effect persuasion through proofs, they do so either with examples or enthymemes; they use nothing else. Accordingly, since all demonstration (as we have shown in the *Analytics*) is effected either by syllogism [that is, deductively] or by induction, it follows that induction and syllogism [deduction] must be identified respectively with example and enthymeme. The difference between example and enthymeme may be inferred from the *Topics*. There, with reference to syllogism [deduction] and induction, it has already been observed that to derive a general law from a number of like instances is in Dialectic induction, in Rhetoric example; whereas to conclude from certain assumptions that something else follows from those assumptions (something distinct from them, yet dependent upon their existing) either universally or as a rule—this in Dialectic is called a syllogism, and in Rhetoric an enthymeme. And of the corresponding two types of oratory it is plain that each has some advantage. What is said of Dialectic in our *Methodology* [a lost work of Aristotle] likewise holds true here; for, of the two kinds of speeches, in one the enthymeme predominates, in the other the example; and similarly some speakers are more given to examples, and others to enthymemes. Arguments through examples are not less persuasive, yet arguments in the form of enthymeme are more applauded. The reason for this, and the right way of using both enthymemes and examples, will be discussed later.

suggestions for discussion and writing

1. What justification does Aristotle have for describing rhetoric as an "art"?

2. Why does Aristotle regard the "enthymeme" and the "example" as "scientific proofs"? What value, if any, does his distinction between "scientific" and "non-scientific" proofs have for the student of rhetoric today?

3. Describe as precisely as you can the relationship that Aristotle sees between "dialectic" and "rhetoric."

4. Give illustrations of what Aristotle means by "enthymeme" and "example."

5. Aristotle's *Rhetoric* has been called an "expanded *Phaedrus*." In this selection, what evidence is there to support this description? Or does this description seem inapplicable?

6. Analyze a speech or a persuasive essay to see whether you can identify examples of the three "means of persuasion" Aristotle enumerates.

7. How can a speaker or writer make his *ethos* a "cause of persuasion"? Give examples of methods he might use.

Marcus Tullius Cicero, lawyer, statesman, and orator, is the foremost example in the ancient world of the rhetorician writing about his art. DE ORATORE, *completed about 55 B.C., is not an original discussion of rhetoric, but a comprehensive statement of its author's mature ideas on the subject. Book I (from which the excerpt below is taken) deals with the function of rhetoric and the education of the orator. Book II discusses the finding and arrangement of subject matter, while Book III elaborates the thesis that style is inseparable from substance.* DE ORATORE *is in the form of a dialogue. Crassus, an illustrious orator and tutor of Cicero, presents Cicero's ideas; Sulpicius and Cotta were both Roman politicians.*

the public responsibilities of the orator

CICERO

IN that place . . . Crassus introduced a conversation on the pursuit of oratory, with a view to relieving all minds from the discourse of the day before. He began by saying that Sulpicius and Cotta seemed not to need exhortation from him but rather commendation, seeing that thus early they had acquired such skill as not merely to be ranked above their equals in age, but to be comparable with their elders. "Moreover," he continued, "there is to my mind no more excellent thing than the power, by means of oratory, to get a hold on assemblies of men, win their good will, direct their inclinations wherever the speaker wishes, or divert them from whatever he wishes. In every free nation, and most of all in communities which have attained the enjoyment of peace and tranquillity, this one art has always flourished above the rest and ever reigned supreme. For what is so marvellous as that, out of the innumerable company of mankind, a single being should arise, who either alone or with a few others can make effective a faculty bestowed by nature upon every man? Or what so pleasing to the understanding and the ear as a speech adorned and polished with wise reflections and dignified language? Or what achievements so mighty and glorious as that the impulses of the crowd, the consciences of the judges, the austerity of the Senate, should suffer transformation through the eloquence of one man? What function again is so kingly, so worthy of the free, so generous, as to bring help to the suppliant, to raise up those that are cast down, to bestow security, to set free from peril, to maintain men in their civil rights? What too is so indispensable as to have always in your grasp weapons wherewith you can defend yourself, or challenge the wicked man, or when provoked take your revenge?

FROM CICERO, *De Oratore,* TRANS. E. W. SUTTON AND H. RACKHAM (2 VOLS.; CAMBRIDGE, MASS.: HARVARD UNIVERSITY PRESS, 1959), I, 23–27. REPRINTED BY PERMISSION OF THE PUBLISHERS AND THE LOEB CLASSICAL LIBRARY.

"Nay more (not to have you for ever contemplating public affairs, the bench, the platform, and the Senatehouse), what in hours of ease can be a pleasanter thing or one more characteristic of culture, than discourse that is graceful and nowhere uninstructed? For the one point in which we have our very greatest advantage over the brute creation is that we hold converse one with another, and can reproduce our thought in word. Who therefore would not rightly admire this faculty, and deem it his duty to exert himself to the utmost in this field, that by so doing he may surpass men themselves in that particular respect wherein chiefly men are superior to animals? To come, however, at length to the highest achievements of eloquence, what other power could have been strong enough either to gather scattered humanity into one place, or to lead it out of its brutish existence in the wilderness up to our present condition of civilization as men and as citizens, or, after the establishment of social communities, to give shape to laws, tribunals, and civic rights? And not to pursue any further instances—wellnigh countless as they are—I will conclude the whole matter in a few words, for my assertion is this: that the wise control of the complete orator is that which chiefly upholds not only his own dignity, but the safety of countless individuals and of the entire State. Go forward therefore, my young friends, in your present course, and bend your energies to that study which engages you, that so it may be in your power to become a glory to yourselves, a source of service to your friends, and profitable members of the Republic."

suggestions for discussion and writing

1. According to Crassus, what specific virtues does the orator have? What does Crassus appear to assume are the principal reasons for knowing how to speak well? What assumptions does Crassus seem to be making about the operations of government?

2. Is Crassus' conception of the orator's role similar to that of Plato or Aristotle or both? How? If you think the conception differs from that of the other two authors, tell how.

3. Given this conception of the orator's role, what sort of education or training do you think the young orator would need?

4. On the basis of this passage, what judgment might Cicero have given of public orators who are prominent today? Select one or two orators of whom Cicero might have approved, and one or two of whom he might have disapproved. Give reasons for your choices.

*A sudden leap of 2,000 years, from 50 B.C. to 1950
A.D., is partly justified by the close attention Kenneth Burke pays to the classical rhetoricians in the
first third of his book,* A RHETORIC OF MOTIVES, *and
the opportunity such a leap gives us to compare
Burke's view of the function of rhetoric with Aristotle's. Rhetoric, for Burke, promotes the* identification *of speaker and hearer. As he suggests a few pages
before the selection below, rhetoric helps to make the
speaker and hearer "consubstantial," that is, it makes
them share part of the same substance (for example,
values, concepts, ideas, attitudes). In all of his works
on rhetoric and literature (which include* COUNTER-
STATEMENT, *1931;* PERMANENCE AND CHANGE, *1935;*
THE PHILOSOPHY OF LITERARY FORM, *1941; and* A
GRAMMAR OF MOTIVES, *1945), Burke is a subtle and
difficult writer, partly because he draws freely on his
wide reading in sociology, anthropology, psychology,
and politics. If the student has difficulty mastering in
detail the selection that follows, he can concentrate
on the definitions of rhetoric it contains and on the
diversity of actions that Burke identifies as "rhetorical."*

rhetoric as a social force

KENNETH BURKE

FROM KENNETH BURKE, *A Rhetoric of Motives* (EN-
GLEWOOD CLIFFS, N. J.: PRENTICE-HALL, INC., 1950),
PP. 38–46. © 1950 BY PRENTICE-HALL, INC. RE-
PRINTED BY PERMISSION OF THE PUBLISHER.

THUS by a roundabout route we come upon another aspect of Rhetoric: its nature as *addressed*, since persuasion implies an audience. A
man can be his own audience, insofar as he, even
in his secret thoughts, cultivates certain ideas or
images for the effect he hopes they may have upon
him; he is here what Mead would call "an 'I' addressing its 'me' "; and in this respect he is being
rhetorical quite as though he were using pleasant
imagery to influence an outside audience rather
than one within. In traditional Rhetoric, the relation to an external audience is stressed. Aristotle's
Art of Rhetoric, for instance, deals with the appeal
to audiences in this primary sense: It lists typical
beliefs, so that the speaker may choose among them
the ones with which he would favorably identify his
cause or unfavorably identify the cause of an opponent; and it lists the traits of character with which
the speaker should seek to identify himself, as a
way of disposing an audience favorably towards
him. But a modern "post-Christian" rhetoric must
also concern itself with the thought that, under the
heading of appeal to audiences, would also be included any ideas or images privately addressed to
the individual self for moralistic or incantatory
purposes. For you become your own audience, in
some respects a very lax one, in some respects
very exacting, when you become involved in psy-
chologically stylistic subterfuges for presenting

your own case to yourself in sympathetic terms (and even terms that seem harsh can often be found on closer scrutiny to be flattering, as with neurotics who visit sufferings upon themselves in the name of very high-powered motives which, whatever their discomfiture, feed pride).

Such considerations make us alert to the ingredient of rhetoric in all *socialization*, considered as a *moralizing* process. The individual person, striving to form himself in accordance with the communicative norms that match the cooperative ways of his society, is by the same token concerned with the rhetoric of identification. To act upon himself persuasively, he must variously resort to images and ideas that are formative. Education ("indoctrination") exerts such pressure upon him from without; he completes the process from within. If he does not somehow act to tell himself (as his own audience) what the various brands of rhetorician have told him, his persuasion is not complete. Only those voices from without are effective which can speak in the language of a voice within.

Among the Tanala of Madagascar, it is said, most of those tribesmen susceptible to *tromba* ("neurotic seizure indicated by an extreme desire to dance") were found to be among the least favored members of the tribe. Such seizures are said to be a device that makes the possessed person "the center of all the attention." And afterwards, the richest and most powerful members of the sufferer's family foot the bill, so that "the individual's ego is well satisfied and he can get along quite well until the next tromba seizure occurs." In sum, "like most hysterical seizures, tromba requires an audience."

The citations are from A. Kardiner, *The Individual and His Society* (New York: Columbia University Press). They would suggest that, when asking what all would fall within the scope of our topic, we could also include a "rhetoric of hysteria." For here too are expressions which are *addressed* —and we confront an ultimate irony, in glimpsing how even a catatonic lapse into sheer automatism, beyond the reach of all normally linguistic communication, is in its origins communicative, addressed, though it be a paralogical appeal-that-ends-all-appeals.

RHETORIC AND PRIMITIVE MAGIC

The Kardiner citations are taken from a paper by

C. Kluckhohn on "Navaho Witchcraft," containing observations that would also bring witchcraft within the range of rhetoric. Indeed, where witchcraft is imputed as a motive behind the individual search for wealth, power, or vengeance, can we not view it as a primitive vocabulary of *individualism* emerging in a culture where *tribal* thinking had been uppermost, so that the individualist motive would be admitted and suspect? And any breach of identification with the tribal norms being sinister, do we not glimpse rhetorical motives behind the fact that Macbeth's private ambitions were figured in terms of witches?

At first glance we may seem to be straining the conception of rhetoric to the breaking point, when including even a treatise on primitive witchcraft within its range. But look again. Precisely at a time when the *term* "rhetoric" had fallen into greatest neglect and disrepute, writers in the "social sciences" were, under many guises, making good contributions to the New Rhetoric. As usual with modern thought, the insights gained from *comparative culture* could throw light upon the classic approach to this subject; and again, as usual with modern thought, this light was interpreted in terms that concealed its true relation to earlier work. And though the present writer was strongly influenced by anthropological inquiries into primitive magic, he did not clearly discern the exact relation between the anthropologist's concern with magic and the literary critic's concern with communication until he had systematically worked on this *Rhetoric* for some years. Prior to this discovery, though he persisted in anthropological hankerings, he did so with a bad conscience; and he was half willing to agree with literary opponents who considered such concerns alien to the study of literature proper.

Now, in noting methodically how the anthropologist's account of magic can belong in a rhetoric, we are better equipped to see exactly wherein the two fields of inquiry diverge. Anthropology is a gain to literary criticism only if one knows how to "discount" it from the standpoint of rhetoric. And, ironically, anthropology can be a source of disturbance, not only to literary criticism in particular, but to the study of human relations in general, if one does not so discount it, but allows *its* terms to creep into one's thinking at points where issues *should* be studied explicitly in terms of rhetoric.

We saw both the respects in which the anthropologists' study of magic overlaps upon rhetoric and the respects in which they are distinct when we were working on a review of Ernst Cassirer's *Myth of the State*. The general proposition that exercised us can be stated as follows:

We must begin by confronting the typically scientist view of the relation between science and magic. Since so many apologists of modern science, following a dialectic of simple antithesis, have looked upon magic merely as an early form of bad science, one seems to be left only with a distinction between bad science and good science. Scientific knowledge is thus presented as a terminology that gives an accurate and critically tested description of reality; and magic is presented as antithetical to such science. Hence magic is treated as an early uncritical attempt to do what science does, but under conditions where judgment and perception were impaired by the naïvely anthropomorphic belief that the impersonal forces of nature were motivated by personal designs. One thus confronts a flat choice between a civilized vocabulary of scientific description and a savage vocabulary of magical incantation.

In this scheme, "rhetoric" has no systematic location. We recall noting the word but once in Cassirer's *Myth of the State*, and then it is used only in a random way; yet the book is really about nothing more nor less than a most characteristic concern of rhetoric: the manipulation of men's beliefs for political ends.

Now, the basic function of rhetoric, the use of words by human agents to form attitudes or to induce actions in other human agents, is certainly not "magical." If you are in trouble, and call for help, you are no practitioner of primitive magic. You are using the primary resource of human speech in a thoroughly realistic way. Nor, on the other hand, is your utterance "science," in the strict meaning of science today, as a "semantic" or "descriptive" terminology for charting the conditions of nature from an "impersonal" point of view, regardless of one's wishes or preferences. A call for help is quite "prejudiced"; it is the most arrant kind of "wishful thinking"; it is not merely descriptive, it is *hortatory*. It is not just trying to tell how things are, in strictly "scenic" terms; it is trying to *move people*. A call for help might, of course, include purely scientific statements, or preparations for action, as a person in need might give information about particular dangers to guard against or advantages to exploit in bringing help. But the call, in itself, as

such, is not scientific; it is *rhetorical*. Whereas poetic language is a kind of symbolic action, for itself and in itself, and whereas scientific action is a preparation for action, rhetorical language is inducement to action (or to attitude, attitude being an incipient act).

If you have only a choice between magic and science, you simply have no bin in which to accurately place such a form of expression. Hence, since "the future" is not the sort of thing one can put under a microscope, or even test by a knowledge of *exactly equivalent conditions* in the past, when you turn to political exhortation, you are involved in decisions that necessarily lie beyond the strictly scientific vocabularies of description. And since the effective politician is a "spellbinder" it seems to follow by elimination that the hortatory use of speech for political ends can be called "magic," in the discredited sense of that term.

As a result, much analysis of political exhortation comes to look simply like a survival of primitive magic, whereas it should be handled in its own terms, as an aspect of what it really is: rhetoric. The approach to rhetoric in terms of "word magic" gets the whole subject turned backwards. Originally, the magical use of symbolism to affect natural processes by rituals and incantations was a mistaken transference of a proper linguistic function to an area for which it was not fit. The realistic use of addressed language to *induce action in people* became the magical use of addressed language to *induce motion in things* (things by nature alien to purely linguistic orders of motivation). If we then begin by treating this *erroneous* and *derived* magical use as *primary*, we are invited to treat a *proper* use of language (for instance, political persuasion) simply as a vestige of benightedly prescientific magic.

To be sure, the rhetorician has the tricks of his trade. But they are not mere "bad science"; they are an "art." And any overly scientist approach to them (treating them in terms of flat dialectical opposition to modern technology) must make our world look much more "neoprimitive" than is really the case. At the very least, we should note that primitive magic prevailed most strongly under social conditions where the rationalization of social effort in terms of money was negligible; but the rhetoric of modern politics would establish social identifications atop a way of life highly diversified by money, with the extreme division of labor and status which money served to rationalize.

REALISTIC FUNCTION OF RHETORIC

Gaining courage as we proceed, we might even contend that we are not so much proposing to import anthropology into rhetoric as proposing that anthropologists recognize the factor of rhetoric in their own field. That is, if you look at recent studies of primitive magic from the standpoint of this discussion, you might rather want to distinguish between magic as "bad science" and magic as "primitive rhetoric." You then discover that anthropology does clearly recognize the rhetorical *function* in magic; and far from dismissing the rhetorical aspect of magic merely as bad science, anthropology recognizes in it a pragmatic device that greatly assisted the survival of cultures by promoting social cohesion. (Malinowski did much work along these lines, and the Kluckhohn essay makes similar observations about witchcraft.) But now that we have confronted the term "magic" with the term "rhetoric," we'd say that one comes closer to the true state of affairs if one treats the socializing aspects of magic as a "primitive rhetoric" than if one sees modern rhetoric simply as a "survival of primitive magic."

For rhetoric as such is not rooted in any past condition of human society. It is rooted in an essential function of language itself, a function that is wholly realistic, and is continually born anew; the use of language as a symbolic means of inducing cooperation in beings that by nature respond to symbols. Though rhetorical considerations may carry us far afield, leading us to violate the principle of autonomy separating the various disciplines, there is an intrinsically rhetorical motive, situated in the persuasive use of language. And this persuasive use of language is not derived from "bad science," or "magic." On the contrary, "magic" was a faulty derivation from it, "word magic" being an attempt to produce linguistic responses in kinds of beings not accessible to the linguistic motive. However, once you introduce this emendation, you can see beyond the accidents of language. You can recognize how much of value has been contributed to the New Rhetoric by these investigators, though their observations are made in terms that never explicitly confront the rhetorical ingredient in their field of study. We can place in terms of rhetoric all those statements by anthropologists, ethnologists, individual and social psychologists, and the like, that bear upon the *persuasive* aspects of language, the function of language as *addressed,* as direct or roundabout appeal to real or ideal audiences, without or within.

Are we but haggling over a term? In one sense, yes. We are offering a rationale intended to show how far one might systematically extend the term "rhetoric." In this respect, we are haggling over a term; for we must persist in tracking down the *function* of that term. But to note the ingredient of rhetoric lurking in such anthropologist's terms as "magic" and "witchcraft" is not to ask that the anthropologist replace his words with ours. We are certainly not haggling over terms in that sense. The term "rhetoric" is no substitute for "magic," "witchcraft," "socialization," "communication," and so on. But the term rhetoric designates a *function* which is present in the areas variously covered by those other terms. And we are asking only that this *function* be recognized for what it is: a linguistic function by nature as *realistic* as a proverb, though it may be quite far from the kind of realism found in strictly "scientific realism." For it is essentially a realism of the *act:* moral, persuasive—and acts are not "true" and "false" in the sense that the propositions of "scientific realism" are. And however "false" the "propositions" of primitive magic may be, considered from the standpoint of scientific realism, it is different with the peculiarly *rhetorical* ingredient in magic, involving ways of identification that contribute variously to social cohesion (either for the advantage of the community as a whole, or for the advantage of special groups whose interests are a burden on the community, or for the advantage of special groups whose rights and duties are indeterminately both a benefit and a tax on the community, as with some business enterprise in our society).

The "pragmatic sanction" for this function of magic lies outside the realm of strictly true-or-false propositions; it falls in an area of deliberation that itself draws upon the resources of rhetoric; it is itself a subject matter belonging to an art that can "prove opposites."

To illustrate what we mean by "proving opposites" here: we read an article, let us say, obviously designed to dispose the reading public favorably towards the "aggressive and expanding" development of American commercial interests in Saudi Arabia. It speaks admiringly of the tremendous changes which our policies of commerce and investment will introduce into a vestigially feudal culture, and of the great speed at which the rationale of finance and technology will accomplish these changes. When considering the obvious rhetorical intent of these "facts," we suddenly, in a perverse *non sequitur*, remember a passage in the Kluckhohn essay, involving what we would now venture to call "the rhetoric of witchcraft":

> In a society like the Navaho which is competitive and capitalistic, on the one hand, and still familistic on the other, any ideology which has the effect of slowing down economic mobility is decidedly adaptive. One of the most basic strains in Navaho society arises out of the incompatibility between the demands of familism and the emulation of European patterns in the accumulating of capital.

And in conclusion we are told that the "survival of the society" is assisted by "any pattern, such as witchcraft, which tends to discourage the rapid accumulation of wealth" (witchcraft, as an "ideology," contributing to this end by identifying new wealth with malign witchery). Now, when you begin talking about the optimum rate of speed at which cultural changes should take place, or the optimum proportion between tribal and individualistic motives that should prevail under a particular set of economic conditions, you are talking about something very important indeed, but you will find yourself deep in matters of rhetoric: for nothing is more rhetorical in nature than a deliberation as to what is too much or too little, too early or too late; in such controversies, rhetoricians are forever "proving opposites."

Where are we now? We have considered two main aspects of rhetoric: its use of *identification* and its nature as *addressed*. Since identification implies division, we found rhetoric involving us in matters of socialization and faction. Here was a wavering line between peace and conflict, since identification is got by property, which is ambivalently a motive of both morality and strife. And inasmuch as the ultimate of conflict is war or murder, we considered how such imagery can figure as a terminology of reidentification ("transformation" or "rebirth"). For in considering the wavering line between identification and division, we shall always be coming upon manifestations of the logomachy, avowed as in invective, unavowed as in stylistic subterfuges for presenting real divisions in terms that deny division.

We found that this wavering line between identification and division was forever bringing rhetoric against the possibility of malice and the lie; for if an identification favorable to the speaker or his cause is made to seem favorable to the audience, there enters the possibility of such "heightened consciousness" as goes with deliberate cunning. Thus, roundabout, we confronted the nature of rhetoric as *addressed* to audiences of the first, second, or third person. Socialization itself was, in the widest sense, found to be addressed. And by reason of such simultaneous identification-with and division-from as mark the choice of a scapegoat, we found that rhetoric involves us in problems related to witchcraft, magic, spellbinding, ethical promptings, and the like. And in the course of discussing these subjects, we found ourselves running into another term: persuasion. Rhetoric is the art of persuasion, or a study of the means of persuasion available for any given situation. We have thus, deviously, come to the point at which Aristotle begins his treatise on rhetoric.

So we shall change our purpose somewhat. Up to now, we have been trying to indicate what kinds of subject matter not traditionally labeled "rhetoric" should, in our opinion, also fall under this head. We would now consider varying views of rhetoric that have already prevailed; and we would try to "generate" them from the same basic terms of our discussion.

As for the relation between "identification" and "persuasion": we might well keep it in mind that a speaker persuades an audience by the use of stylistic identifications; his act of persuasion may be for the purpose of causing the audience to identify itself with the speaker's interests; and the speaker draws on identification of interests to establish rapport between himself and his audience. So, there is no chance of our keeping apart the meanings of persuasion, identification ("consubstantiality") and communication (the nature of rhetoric as "addressed"). But, in given instances, one or another of these elements may serve best for extending a line of analysis in some particular direction.

And finally: The use of symbols, by one symbol-using entity to induce action in another (persuasion properly addressed) is in essence not magical but *realistic*. However, the resources of identification whereby a sense of consubstantiality is symbolically established between beings of unequal status may extend far into the realm of the *idealistic*. And as we shall see later, when on the subject of order, out of this idealistic element there may arise a kind of magic or mystery that sets its mark upon all human relations.

suggestions for discussion and writing

1. On what fields of knowledge does Burke draw in this discussion of the workings of rhetoric? (One can add contemporary psychology, for the paragraph preceding this selection alludes to Freud's *Wit and Its Relation to the Unconscious.*)

2. In what sense can witchcraft and magic be called kinds of rhetoric?

3. What assumptions does Burke appear to be making about the social functions of rhetoric?

4. What do you think Burke means when he describes the use of language as "realistic"?

5. Would you say that Burke defines rhetoric differently from Aristotle? from Plato? Wherein do the differences lie? In the number of acts described as rhetorical? In other features? Explain.

6. What does Burke mean in reiterating Aristotle's statement that rhetoric can "prove opposites," and why is this power valuable?

7. Mention some examples of social behavior or activities (other than writing) that you have observed or read about that seem to you to fall within Burke's definition of rhetoric. Explain why you think these examples may fit the definition.

8. Examine a current speech or persuasive essay, identify features of the language that seem intended to assist the "identification" of audience and speaker, and say why you think they are so intended.

Although Kenneth Burke and others included in this collection are university teachers, none exemplifies the professional twentieth-century scholar of rhetoric and public address nearly so well as Dr. Bryant. For many years professor of speech at the University of Iowa, author of a text on public speaking, contributor to professional periodicals, and former editor of the QUARTERLY JOURNAL OF SPEECH, *Dr. Bryant is one of many teachers of speech who have kept alive an interest in rhetorical theory and practice in American universities. The excerpts that follow come from a long essay that seeks to define rhetoric (more conventionally perhaps than Burke does) and to identify the unique values of the discipline for thinking adults of the twentieth century.*

rhetoric: its functions and its scope

DONALD C. BRYANT

ARISTOTLE'S system, therefore, and his rationale of effective speaking comprehend with very little violence the art of the good man skilled in speaking of Cicero and Quintilian, or Baldwin's equation of rhetoric to the art of prose whose end is giving effectiveness to truth[1]—effectiveness considered in terms of what happens to an audience, usually a popular or lay audience as distinguished from the specialized or technical audience of the scientific or dialectical demonstration. This distinction, strictly speaking, is a practical rather than a logical limitation, a limitation of degree rather than kind. No matter what the audience, when the speaker evinces skill in getting into their minds, he evinces rhetorical skill.

If the breadth of scope which I have assigned to rhetoric is implicit in Aristotle's system, the basic delimitation of that scope finds early and explicit statement there. Rhetoric is not confined in application to any specific subjects which are exclusively its own. Rhetoric is method, not subject. But if it has no special subjects, neither are all subjects within its province. In its suasory phase, at least, rhetoric is concerned, said Aristotle, only with those questions about which men dispute, that is, with the contingent—that which is dependent in part upon factors which cannot be known for certain, that which can be otherwise. Men do not dispute about what is known or certainly knowable by them. Hence the characteristic concern of rhetoric is broadly with questions of justice and injustice, of the expedient and the inexpedient (of the desirable and undesirable, of the good and the bad), of praise and blame, or honor and dishonor.

To questions such as these and their almost in-

[1] *Ancient Rhetoric and Poetic* (New York, 1924), p. 5.

FROM THE *Quarterly Journal of Speech,* DECEMBER 1953, PP. 404–407, 411–413. REPRINTED BY PERMISSION OF THE SPEECH ASSOCIATION OF AMERICA AND DONALD C. BRYANT.

finite subsidiary questions, vital and perennial as they are in the practical operation of human society, the best answers can never be certain but only more or less probable. In reasoning about them, men at best must usually proceed from probable premise to probable conclusion, seldom from universal to universal. Hence Aristotle described the basic instrument of rhetoric, the enthymeme, as a kind of syllogism based on probabilities and signs.

Rhetoric, therefore, is distinguished from the other instrumental studies in its preoccupation with informed opinion rather than with scientific demonstration. It is the counterpart, said Aristotle, of dialectic. Strictly speaking, dialectic also may be said to attain only probability, not scientific certainty, like physics (and, perhaps, theology). The methodology, however, is the methodology of formal logic and it deals in universals. Hence it arrives at a very high degree of probability, for it admits the debatable only in the assumption of its premises. Rhetoric, however, because it normally deals with matters of uncertainty for the benefit of popular audiences, must admit probability not only in its premises but in its method also. This is the ground upon which Plato first, and hundreds of critics since, have attacked rhetoric—that it deals with opinion rather than knowledge. This is the ground also from which certain scholars have argued,[2] after some of the mediaeval fathers, that rhetoric really deals, characteristically, not with genuine probability but only with adumbration and suggestion. It is, they say, distinguished from dialectic in *degree* of probability—dialectic very high, and rhetoric very low.

The epistemological question is interesting, and in a world of philosophers where only certain knowledge was ever called upon to decide questions of human behavior, it would be the central question. Rhetoric exists, however, because a world of certainty is not the world of human affairs. It exists because the world of human affairs is a world where there must be an alternative to certain knowledge on the one hand and pure chance or whimsey on the other. The alternative is informed opinion, the nearest approach to knowledge which the circumstances of decision in any given case will permit. The art, or science, or method whose realm this is, is rhetoric. Rhetoric, therefore, is the

method, the strategy, the organon of the principles for deciding best the undecidable questions, for arriving at solutions of the unsolvable problems, for instituting method in those vital phases of human activity where no method is inherent in the total subject-matter of decision. The resolving of such problems is the province of the "Good man skilled in speaking." It always has been, and it is still. Of that there can be little question. And the comprehensive rationale of the functioning of the good man so far as he is skilled in speaking, so far as he is a wielder of public opinion, is rhetoric. . . .

RELATIONS OF RHETORIC TO OTHER LEARNINGS

These, then, are fundamental rhetorical situations. In them human beings are so organizing language as to effect a change in the knowledge, the understanding, the ideas, the attitudes, or the behavior of other human beings. Furthermore, they are so organizing that language as to make the change as agreeable, as easy, as active, and as secure as possible—as the Roman rhetoric had it, to teach, to delight, and to move (or to bend). What makes a situation rhetorical is the focus upon accomplishing something predetermined and directional with an audience. To that end many knowledges and sciences, concerning both what is external to audiences and what applies to audiences themselves, may be involved, many of which I have discussed in a previous essay.[3] These knowledges, however, have to be organized, managed, given places in strategy and tactics, set into coordinated and harmonious movement towards the listener as the end, towards what happens to him and in him. In short, they have to be *put to use,* for, as Bacon said, studies themselves "teach not their own use; but that is a wisdom without them, and above them, won by observation." "Studies themselves do give forth directions too much at large, except they be bounded in by experience."[4] Rhetoric teaches their use towards a particular end. It is that "observation," that "experience" codified, given a rationale. Other learnings are chiefly concerned with the discovery of ideas and phenomena and of their relations to each other within more or less homogeneous and closed systems. Rhetoric is primarily concerned with the relations of ideas to the thoughts, feelings, motives, and behavior of

[2] For example, Craig La Drière, "Rhetoric as 'Merely Verbal' Art," *English Institute Essays—1948,* ed. by D. A. Robertson, Jr. (New York, 1949), pp. 123–152.

[3] "Aspects of the Rhetorical Tradition" (1950).
[4] "Of Studies."

men. Rhetoric as distinct from the learnings which it uses is dynamic; it is concerned with movement. It *does* rather than *is*. It is method rather than matter. It is chiefly involved with bringing about a condition, rather than discovering or testing a condition. Even psychology, which is more nearly the special province of rhetoric than is any other study, is descriptive of conditions, but not of the uses of those conditions.

So far as it is method, rhetoric is like the established procedures of experimental science and like logic. As the method for solving problems of human action in the areas of the contingent and the probable, however, it does not enjoy a privilege which is at the same time the great virtue and the great limitation of science and logic—it cannot choose its problems in accordance with the current capacities of its method, or defer them until method is equal to the task. Rhetoric will postpone decision as long as feasible; indeed one of its most valuable uses in the hands of good men, is to prevent hasty and premature formulation of lines of conduct and decision. In this it is one with science —and good sense. But in human affairs, where the whole is usually greater than the most complete collection of the parts, decisions—makings up of the mind—cannot always wait until all the contingencies have been removed and solutions to problems have been tested in advance. Rhetoric, therefore, must take undemonstrable problems and do its best with them when decision is required. We must decide when the blockade is imposed whether to withdraw from Berlin or to undertake the air lift, not some time later when perhaps some of the contingencies may have been removed. And the making of the choice forever precludes trying out and testing the other possibilities under the circumstances which would have prevailed had we chosen differently at first. Likewise we must make a choice on the first Tuesday in November, whether we are scientifically sure or not. In each case, rhetoric, good or bad, must be the strategy of enlightening opinion for that choice.

To restate our central idea still another way: rhetoric, or the rhetorical, is the function in human affairs which governs and gives direction to that creative activity, that process of critical analysis, that branch of learning, which address themselves to the whole phenomenon of the designed use of language for the promulgation of information, ideas, and attitudes. Though it is instrumental in the discovery of ideas and information, its character-

istic function is the publication, the publicizing, the humanizing, the animating of them for a realized and usually specific audience. At its best it seeks the "energizing of truth," in order to make "reason and the will of God prevail." But except in science, and no doubt theology, the promulgation of *truth,* sure or demonstrable, is out of the question. Normally the rhetorical function serves as high a degree of probability as the combination of subject, audience, speaker, and occasion admits. Rhetoric may or may not be involved (though the speaker-writer must be) in the determination of the validity of the ideas being promulgated. Such determination will be the province in any given situation of philosophy, ethics, physics, economics, politics, eugenics, medicine, hydraulics, or bucolics. To rhetoric, however, and to no other rationale, belongs the efficiency—the validity if you will— of the relations in the idea-audience-speaker situation.

FUNCTIONING OF RHETORIC

We are ready now, perhaps, if we have not been ready much sooner, to proceed to the question of how rhetoric works, what it accomplishes in an audience. Speaking generally, we may say that the rhetorical function is the *function of adjusting ideas to people and people to ideas*. This process may be thought of as a continuum from the complete modification or accommodation of ideas to audiences (as is sometimes said, "telling people only what they want to hear") at the one extreme, to complete regeneration at the other (such perfect illumination that the "facts speak for themselves"). This continuum may, therefore, be said to have complete flattery (to use Plato's unflattering epithet) at one end and the Kingdom of Heaven at the other! Good rhetoric usually functions somewhere well in from the extremes. There, difficult and strange ideas have to be modified without being distorted or invalidated; and audiences have to be prepared through the mitigation of their prejudices, ignorance, and irrelevant sets of mind without being dispossessed of their judgments. The adjustment of ideas to people, for example, was being undertaken by the Earl of Chatham in his speech for the repeal of the Stamp Act, when he agreed that Parliament had legislative supremacy over the Colonies but that legislative supremacy did not include the right to tax without representation. And when Booker T. Washington assured the Southern white folk that they and the Negroes could be as separate as the fingers in social affairs and as united as the hand in economic, he was adjusting people to the idea of real freedom for his race. . . .

suggestions for discussion and writing

1. Since Dr. Bryant's definition of rhetoric is not entirely derived from that of Plato, Aristotle, and Cicero, what new conceptions of rhetoric does he introduce?

2. What assumptions does Dr. Bryant make about the character and motives of the practitioner of rhetoric? Would Plato and Aristotle make the same assumptions? Why or why not?

3. Like Cicero and Burke, Dr. Bryant finds in rhetoric a social usefulness. Does he agree with Cicero and Burke on what that social usefulness is, or does he perceive it differently? How do you know?

4. Paraphrase in your own words what Dr. Bryant means when he says "[Rhetoric] is method rather than matter."

5. Is the scope of rhetoric, as Dr. Bryant sees it, wide enough to include imaginative literature? In Bryant's definition, would we call imaginative literature "rhetorical"? Defend your answer.

6. Mention some subject that would be appropriate for the practice of the rhetorician's art, as Dr. Bryant describes it. Mention some subjects which the rhetorician would not be likely to treat. Give reasons for your choices.

7. What procedures in the analysis of issues and in the gathering and interpretation of data does the rhetorician need to employ if he hopes to live up to Dr. Bryant's characterization of him? In other words, does Bryant's definition of rhetoric imply that the rhetorician will have to conduct his research and analysis in a distinctive way? Why or why not?

The scholarly interests of Dr. Steinmann, who is professor of English at the University of Minnesota, include logic, literary criticism, and the English language, in addition to rhetoric. Like Donald Bryant (and Robert Gorrell, Francis Christensen, and Josephine Miles, whose writings appear in the following pages), Steinmann belongs to the group of college teachers of rhetoric and composition who are reviving the study of rhetoric today and contributing to the development of new rhetorical theories. In the passage that follows, he gives a definition of "rhetoric"; he then goes on to argue (in a discussion not given here) that no adequate research has yet been undertaken to find ways of evaluating rhetorical theories, or to explain the effectiveness or ineffectiveness of the "exercise of rhetorical ability" (by which he presumably means the performance) of a writer or speaker.

a modern definition of rhetoric

MARTIN STEINMANN, JR.

To say precisely what rhetoric is, I must first distinguish two senses of "knowing" easily confused in discussing any discipline having human behavior as its object and then describe the three things of which one must have knowledge if one is to use a language effectively.

There are two senses of "knowing": knowing *how* and knowing *that*. In the first sense, a person is said to know something (a language, say) if he possesses a certain ability, if he can perform in certain ways (speak the language). He has knowledge because he knows *how* to do something. In the second sense, he is said to know something (a language, say) if he possesses either a theory (of grammar and semantics) explaining exercise of a certain ability (speaking the language) or information about some historically given events (certain utterances). He has knowledge because he knows *that* something is the case. Neither sort of knowledge entails the other (thousands of American four-year-olds know English in the first sense but not in the second, and thousands of American adults know some French in the second sense but not in the first). (Cf. Gilbert Ryle, *The Concept of Mind* [London, 1949], ch. 2; W. N. Francis, "Language and Linguistics in the English Program," *College English,* 26 [1964], 14.)

To use a language effectively—to speak or write English, say—one must have, in the *first* sense, knowledge of three things.

First, to speak or write at all, one must know English; that is, know *how* to choose between English and non-English expressions. To know

FROM MARTIN STEINMANN, JR., "RHETORICAL RESEARCH," *College English,* JANUARY 1966, PP. 278–281. REPRINTED BY PERMISSION OF THE NATIONAL COUNCIL OF TEACHERS OF ENGLISH AND MARTIN STEINMANN, JR.

English is to possess the ability to make one's utterances conform to a set of rules—grammatical (concerned with form) and semantic (concerned with meaning and including the rules of deductive logic)—that decide for a given expression whether it is English. These rules do not uniquely determine one's utterances; they simply restrict his range of choice.

Second, to speak or write effectively, one must know *how* to think effectively; that is, know *how* to choose wisely between things to say, between *non*synonymous expressions.

If expressions differ in form (in sounds or sequences of sounds or in characters or sequences of characters) but not in meaning (a certain sort of relation between form and other things), they are synonymous; if they differ in both form and meaning, nonsynonymous. Every difference in meaning entails a difference in form, but not every difference in form entails a difference in meaning. Meaning is inseparable from form, but several forms may have the same meaning: the height of the Empire State Building is inseparable from the Empire State Building, but other buildings may have the same height.

As Gilbert Ryle has shown *(The Concept of Mind),* to think is to choose between nonsynonymous expressions; thought and expression are inseparable; having a thought and giving it some expression—in English or Turkish, say, or (since not all expressions are utterances) in a diagram—are not distinct, successive activities. One does not conceive a theory and then express it; he conceives it by expressing it; and, if he cannot express it, he doesn't have it. One does not solve a jig-saw puzzle and then express his solution; he solves it by expressing his solution, by fitting the pieces together correctly or, at least subvocally, giving an account of how they may be correctly fitted together; and, if he can't do this, he doesn't have a solution. A thought too deep for expression is not a thought. . . . And, of course, not all of one's responses, verbal or otherwise, are thoughts or expressions of thoughts. Conditioned responses—recitation of maxims, cocktail-party chatter, selection of the right gear, or shaking hands—are neither thoughts nor expressions of thoughts. But most utterances are not conditioned responses, for most utterances are unique. Indeed, this very sentence—"But most utterances are not conditioned responses, for most utterances are unique"—has probably never been uttered before and, except (as now)

within quotation marks, will probably never be uttered again. The creativity that produces (and understands) unique utterances, often noted by Noam Chomsky (e.g., review of Skinner's *Verbal Behavior, Language,* 35 [1959], 26-58), is the creativity of thought.

Third, to speak or write effectively, one must know rhetoric; that is, know *how* to choose wisely between ways of saying the same thing, between synonymous expressions.

Though thought and expression are inseparable, it makes sense to say that someone expresses a thought effectively and to hold that, in saying this, we refer to three distinct things: *(a)* a certain person, *(b)* a certain thought, and *(c)* a certain expression of *(b).* The mistake lies, not in holding this, but in imagining that *(b)* and *(c)* are separable—that, for example, *(b)* is some sort of *event* occurring *within (a),* a thought-thinking that causes *(c),* say, or of which *(c)* is a good description or photograph. For every description of this mysterious event turns out to be either identical or synonymous with *(c).* "*(a),*" we remark, "certainly expressed his thought effectively when he said, 'Taxation without representation is tyranny.' " But, if we are asked what thought *(a)* expressed when he said that, we are puzzled by the question and can only reply, "Why, the thought that taxation without representation is tyranny" or "The thought that an un- or disfranchised taxpayer is unfairly put upon." And, if *(a)* himself is asked this question, he can do no better. The fact is, of course, that, far from being an event occurring *within (a), (b)* is not an event at all, but a relation, and not a relation *within (a)* or even between *(a)* and something else, but a relation between *(c)* and something else. In other words, *(b)* is a meaning—a certain sort of relation between *(c),* a form, and something else. A thought is a meaning; and it makes sense to say that someone expresses his meaning effectively and to hold that, in saying this, we refer to three distinct things: *(a)* a certain person, *(b)* a certain *meaning,* and *(c)* a certain expression of *(b).* Meaning is inseparable from form, in the way that cousinage is inseparable from cousins. But, as we have seen, several forms may have the same meaning, several expressions may be synonymous; what is more, some of these synonymous expressions may be *rhetorically* more effective than others.

Rhetoric, then, is concerned with the effective choice of synonymous expressions; but, as the word "effective" suggests, it is concerned, not with utterances only, the mere forms, but with some of their relations to other things. These other things are among the six variables that every act of speech or writing has: the speaker or writer, his utterance, his context (occasion or medium), his audience (listener or reader), his purpose (the effect that he intends his utterance to have upon his audience), and the effect of his utterance upon his audience; and rhetoric is best characterized by reference to these variables.

Rhetorical knowledge in the *first* sense (the knowing-*how* sense) is rhetorical ability—the ability of a speaker or writer to speak or write effectively *insofar as effectiveness can result from (a) his choice of synonymous expressions and (b) his control of those other variables that are within his control.* His choice of *non*synonymous expressions is exercise, not of his rhetorical ability, but of his ability to think; and not all the other variables are within his control. Sometimes, though not always, he can choose his context, his audience, and his purpose; but, obviously, he can never choose to be a different person, another speaker or writer. Granted these qualifications, rhetorical knowledge in the first sense is, then, the ability of a speaker or writer to do such a thing as adapting his utterance to his context, his audience, and his purpose—or adapting his utterance, his context, and his audience to his purpose—and thus producing the response that his purpose calls for.

Rhetorical knowledge in the *second* sense (the knowing-*that* sense) is not an ability (or skill or art) at all, but either a well-confirmed rhetorical theory (explaining either exercise of rhetorical ability or something closely related to it) or a body of rhetorical information (about either historically given utterances or historically given rhetorical theories).

This definition of "rhetoric," though similar to the classical one, is at once broader and narrower. On the one hand, it makes writing as well as speaking (oratory) part of the province of rhetoric; and it does not identify rhetorical effectiveness with successful persuasion but with all successful uses of language. By this definition, successful persuasion is only one sort of rhetorical effectiveness; successful communication of knowledge, for example, is another sort, perhaps the most important. On the other hand, this definition excludes both invention (choosing between nonsynonymous expressions) and memory from the province of rhetoric—retaining arrangement, expression, and delivery (choosing between synonymous expressions)—and it excludes also moral or ethical choices. Central to both definitions, however, is the concept of effective expression: "rhetoric . . . . erit bene dicendi scientia"[1] (Quintilian, *Institutio Oratoria* III.iii.12); and, though classical rhetoric embraced much, it emphasized expression, style (e.g., *Institutio* VIII.Pr. 16–17).

[1] Rhetoric is the science of speaking well [Ed.].

suggestions for discussion and writing

1. How does Steinmann's definition of "rhetoric" differ in emphasis from that of Aristotle? of Donald Bryant?

2. Restate in your own words, to be sure that you understand it, Steinmann's distinction between thinking, on the one hand, and choosing ways of expressing that thought, on the other. Give examples to illustrate the distinction.

3. Are there such things as truly "synonymous" expressions? Give examples of expressions you think may be synonymous, and then discuss them to see whether they are different in meaning. If you think it difficult to find truly "synonymous" expressions, might you conclude that to choose among different possible expressions really requires a choice among thoughts rather than just finding the expression that is most effective rhetorically?

4. What are some possible sources of difference in the rhetorical effectiveness of different expressions? Wherein might rhetorical "effectiveness" lie?

5. Do the twentieth-century writers on language and style in the third section of this collection appear to be working with a definition of rhetoric similar to that of Steinmann? Give evidence to support your views.

6. In this essay Steinmann explicitly separates the provinces of "logic" and "rhetoric." Other writers, among them the philosopher Monroe Beardsley, argue that logic and rhetoric cannot be separated, and that one cannot be said to argue well unless he has a good (logically sound) argument. What is your position on this issue? Explain and defend it.

Although the RHETORIC *is still valued as an instructional text for speakers and writers, Aristotle's purpose in it was evidently taxonomic—to gather, classify, and record for his students what was known in his time about the kinds of discourse and the strategies and argument that would persuade. The selection below gives his division of rhetorical discourse into classes, and four of his discussions of "topoi"—sources of argument or ways of bringing data together in support of arguments.*

some
sources
of
argument

ARISTOTLE

THERE are three kinds of speeches in Rhetoric, *1* deliberative, *2* forensic, and *3* epideictic. [That is, there are *1* speeches of counsel or advice (deliberation)—as political speeches addressed to an assembly or to the public on questions of State, but also, for example, a speech addressed to an individual (a ruler, or, indeed, any person who is to be advised); *2* judicial speeches, used in prosecution and defence (more generally, in any kind of attack or defence); and *3* panegyrical or declamatory speeches, in the nature of an exhibition or display, eulogies—in general, speeches of praise (or blame).]

1 The elements of deliberation [counsel] are *(a)* exhortation [encouragement], *(b)* dissuasion; for, as advice given in private always has one or the other aspect, so is it with those who discuss matters of State in public—they either exhort or dissuade. *2* The elements of forensic speaking are *(a)* accusation, *(b)* defence, since the parties to a legal action will necessarily be engaged in either one or the other. *3* The elements of an epideictic speech are *(a)* praise and *(b)* blame. . . .

For these three kinds of Rhetoric there are also three several ends. *1* The aim of the deliberative speaker concerns advantage and injury; for the one who exhorts recommends a course of action as better, and the one who dissuades deters us from it as worse; other considerations—of justice and injustice, of honor and dishonor—he makes subsidiary to this end [of the expedient]. *2* The aim of judicial pleaders concerns justice and injustice, and they in like manner make the other considerations subsidiary to these. *3* The aim of those who praise and blame concerns honor and dishonor, and such speakers likewise subordinate the other considerations to these.

. . .

[One] *topos* is that *a fortiori* [from degrees of more and less]. Thus you may argue that if not even the gods are omniscient, much less are men;

FROM *The Rhetoric of Aristotle*, TRANS. LANE COOPER (NEW YORK: APPLETON-CENTURY-CROFTS, INC., 1960), PP. 17–18, 161, 163–164, 166. COPYRIGHT 1932, 1960 BY LANE COOPER. REPRINTED BY PERMISSION OF APPLETON-CENTURY-CROFTS. MATERIAL WITHIN BRACKETS HAS BEEN INTERPOLATED BY THE TRANSLATOR IN ORDER TO EXPLAIN OCCASIONALLY CRYPTIC PASSAGES AND REFERENCES IN THE TEXT.

on the principle that, if a thing cannot be found where it is more likely to exist, of course you will not find it where it is less likely. Again, you may argue that a man who strikes his father will also strike his neighbors; on the principle that, if the less frequent thing occurs, then the more frequent thing occurs—for people strike their fathers less frequently than they strike their neighbors. . . .

. . .

Another *topos* is from definition. Thus [Socrates in Plato's *Apology* 27 c–e defines his term]: "What is 'the divine'? It must be either a god or the work of a god. Well, then, any one who believes in the existence of a work of a god must needs believe in the existence of gods." So Iphicrates [in meeting the charge of lowly birth defines and argues]: " 'True nobility' is *goodness*. There was nothing noble about Harmodius and Aristogeiton until they had done a noble deed." And he argues further that he himself is more akin [to those heroes than his adversary (a contemporary Harmodius) is]: "At any rate, my deeds are more akin to those of Harmodius and Aristogeiton than yours are." Another example is found in the [*Apology for*] *Paris* [(?) by Polycrates]: "We shall all admit that by 'incontinent' people we mean those who are not content with the enjoyment of one

love." [And Paris was content with Helen.] Or take the reason Socrates gave for not visiting the court of Archelaus: " 'Ignominy' consists as much in not being able to repay a benefit as in not being able to requite an evil." Each of the persons mentioned defines his term, gets at its essential meaning, and then proceeds to reason from it on the point at issue.

. . .

Another *topos* is from [logical] division. Thus you may argue: "All men do wrong from one of three motives, A, B, C. In my case, the first two of these motives are out of the question; and as for the third, C, the prosecution itself does not allege this."

. . .

Another *topos* is from consequences. Since it commonly happens that a given thing has consequences both good and bad, you may argue from these [to their antecedents] in urging or dissuading, in prosecuting or defending, in praising or blaming. For example: education results in unpopularity, a bad consequence, and in wisdom, a good consequence. And so you may argue: It is not well to be educated, since it is not well to be unpopular. Or: It is well to be educated, since it is well to be wise. . . .

suggestions for discussion and writing

1. Is Aristotle's division of the kinds of rhetoric still applicable today? Are any kinds of discourse frequent today that cannot be fitted into one of Aristotle's three classes? Give a modern example of a member of each of his classes.

2. In the writing (or speech) courses that you have had to date, have you practiced each of the three kinds of discourse Aristotle identifies? If not, do you think you should have practiced each of the three? Why or why not?

3. Give an example from a modern writer for each of the "topoi" mentioned in this selection. What other "topoi," or sources of argument, appear frequently in

twentieth-century writing? Is it useful to analyze contemporary speeches and essays in terms of "topoi"— Aristotelian or other? Explain your position.

4. Do the four "topoi" amplify or confuse your understanding of what Aristotle means by an "enthymeme"? How?

5. Construct an argumentative paper for each of Aristotle's three classifications of discourse. In each paper use all "topoi" discussed here. Then consider: would your handling of the subject have been appreciably different if you had *not* been making deliberate use of the "topoi"?

Although DE INVENTIONE *was written in Cicero's youth, some thirty years before* DE ORATORE, *and although it is mostly a compendium of theories of earlier Greek and Roman teachers, this work is of value to the modern student of rhetoric, in part for its detailed discussion of the form of an oration (an emphasis Cicero himself seems later to have regretted). Readers should consider whether the model presented here—in broad outline, with most details eliminated for lack of space—is in any respects an accurate description of modern practices in the construction of formal oral and written discourses, and whether knowing this model can be helpful to students of writing and speaking today.*

the organization of a speech

CICERO

THEREFORE when the point for decision and the arguments which must be devised for the purpose of reaching a decision have been diligently discovered by the rules of art, and studied with careful thought, then, and not till then, the other parts of the oration are to be arranged in proper order. These seem to me to be just six in number: exordium, narrative, partition, confirmation, refutation, peroration.

Now since the exordium has to come first, we shall likewise give first the rule for a systematic treatment of the exordium. An exordium is a passage which brings the mind of the auditor into a proper condition to receive the rest of the speech. This will be accomplished if he becomes well-disposed, attentive, and receptive. Therefore one who wishes his speech to have a good exordium must make a careful study beforehand of the kind of case which he has to present. . . .

. . .

The *narrative* is an exposition of events that have occurred or are supposed to have occurred. There are three kinds: one which contains just the case and the whole reason for the dispute; a second in which a digression is made beyond the strict limits of the case for the purpose of attacking somebody, or of making a comparison, or of amusing the audience in a way not incongruous with the business in hand, or for amplification. The third kind is wholly unconnected with public issues, which is recited or written solely for amusement but at the same time provides valuable training. It is subdivided into two classes: one concerned with events, the other principally with persons. . . .

. . .

[The] narrative . . . of a case at law ought to

FROM CICERO, *De Inventione*, TRANS. H. M. HUBBELL (CAMBRIDGE, MASS.: HARVARD UNIVERSITY PRESS, 1960), PP. 41, 55, 57, 63, 69–71, 123, 125, 147. REPRINTED BY PERMISSION OF THE PUBLISHERS AND THE LOEB CLASSICAL LIBRARY.

possess three qualities: it should be brief, clear, and plausible.

. . .

Let us now pass to the *partition*. In an argument a partition correctly made renders the whole speech clear and perspicuous. It takes two forms, both of which greatly contribute to clarifying the case and determining the nature of the controversy. One form shows in what we agree with our opponents and what is left in dispute; as a result of this some definite problem is set for the auditor on which he ought to have his attention fixed. In the second form the matters which we intend to discuss are briefly set forth in a methodical way. This leads the auditor to hold definite points in his mind, and to understand that when these have been discussed the oration will be over.

. . .

Now it seems desirable to give in turn the rules about *confirmation* as is demanded by the regular order of the speech. Confirmation or proof is the part of the oration which by marshalling arguments lends credit, authority, and support to our case. For this section of the speech there are definite rules which will be divided among the different kinds of cases. But I think that it will not be inconvenient to set forth in the beginning . . . a kind of raw material for general use from which all arguments are drawn. . . .

All propositions are supported in argument by attributes of persons or of actions. We hold the following to be the attributes of persons: name, nature, manner of life, fortune, habit, feeling, interests, purposes, achievements, accidents, speeches made. [Among attributes of actions, Cicero lists the name, means of performance, and motive for the act; the events that preceded the act, the details of how the act was performed, and the events that followed the act; the place, time, and occasion for performance of the act; the state of mind of the doer when he performed the act; similarities and differences between the act and comparable acts; and the consequences of the act.]. . .

The *refutation* is that part of an oration in which arguments are used to impair, disprove, or weaken the confirmation or proof in our opponents' speech. It utilizes the same sources of invention that *confirmation* does, because any proposition can be attacked by the same methods of reasoning by which it can be supported. . . .

. . .

Every argument is refuted in one of these ways: either one or more of its assumptions are not granted, or if the assumptions are granted it is denied that a conclusion follows from them, or the form of argument is shown to be fallacious, or a strong argument is met by one equally strong or stronger.

. . .

The peroration is the end and conclusion of the whole speech; it has three parts, the summing-up, the *indignatio* or exciting of indignation or ill-will against the opponent, and the *conquestio* or the arousing of pity and sympathy.

suggestions for discussion and writing

1. Analyze any piece of formal discourse to see whether you can observe any of the six parts of the classical oration as Cicero describes it.

2. Examine your own practice in composing argumentative papers. Do you follow, unconsciously, any of the procedures Cicero enumerates? Would your papers be improved if you did? Why or why not?

3. Write an argumentative composition that contains the six parts Cicero enumerates. Then criticize your composition: is it a convincing presentation of the arguments on the issue you are discussing?

4. In suggesting the six-part design for an argument, what striking assumptions, if any, does Cicero seem to make about the goals to be sought in composing discourse and about the attitudes or interests of those who listen to or read discourse? Are these assumptions, if made in general terms, fair guides for the speaker or writer to use in practice?

*Marcus Fabius Quintilianus, son of a well-known
rhetorician, was a prosperous lawyer and a teacher
of rhetoric in a state-supported public school in
Rome. Designed apparently for teachers as well as
for students of rhetoric, his* INSTITUTES OF ORATORY,
*completed near the end of the first century A.D., is a
long review of knowledge and theories about rhetoric available in his day. A distinguishing feature
of his work is his insistence that rhetorical invention
requires careful investigation and analysis of the
issues with which the speaker or writer is dealing. In
the following brief excerpts he urges the speaker to
determine the "basis"—the central question or issue
in a dispute—before attempting to develop his arguments.*

determining the central issue

QUINTILIAN

E VERY question has its *basis,* since every question is based on assertion by one party and
denial by another. . . .

. . .

A simple cause, however, although it may be
defended in various ways, cannot have more than
one point on which a decision has to be given, and
consequently the *basis* of the cause will be that
point which the orator sees to be the most important
for him to make and on which the judge sees that
he must fix all his attention. For it is on this that
the cause will stand or fall. On the other hand
questions may have more *bases* than one. A brief
example will show what I mean. When the ac-
cused says "Admitting that I did it, I was right to
do it," he makes the *basis* one of *quality;* but when
he adds "but I did not do it," he introduces an element of *conjecture.* But denial of the facts is always
the stronger line of defence, and therefore I conceive the *basis* to reside in that which I should
say, if I were confined to one single line of argument. . . .

. . .

We must therefore accept the view of the
authorities followed by Cicero, to the effect that
there are three things on which enquiry is made in
every case: we ask *whether a thing is, what it is,* and
of what kind it is. Nature herself imposes this upon
us. For first of all there must be some subject for
the question, since we cannot possibly determine
what a thing is, or *of what kind it is,* until we have
first ascertained *whether it is,* and therefore the
first question raised is *whether it is.* But even when
it is clear that a thing *is,* it is not immediately obvious *what it is.* And when we have decided what
it is, there remains the question of its *quality.* These

FROM QUINTILIAN, *Institutio Oratoria,* TRANS. H. E.
BUTLER (4 VOLS.; CAMBRIDGE, MASS.: HARVARD UNI-
VERSITY PRESS, 1958), I, 411, 413, 451, 463. RE-
PRINTED BY PERMISSION OF THE PUBLISHERS AND THE
LOEB CLASSICAL LIBRARY.

three points once ascertained, there is no further question to ask. These heads cover both *definite* and *indefinite questions.*[1] One or more of them is discussed in every demonstrative, deliberative or forensic theme. These heads again cover all cases in the courts, whether we regard them from the point of view of *rational* or *legal questions.* For

[1] A *definite* question is one that refers to a particular person or time. An *indefinite* question is abstract, unrelated to a specific person or time.

no legal problem can be settled save by the aid of *definition, quality* and *conjecture.* . . .

.   .   .

Every kind of case will contain a *cause point for the decision of the judge,* and a *central argument.* For nothing can be said which does not contain a reason, something to which the decision of the judge is directed, and finally something which, more than aught else, contains the substancy of the matter at issue.

suggestions for discussion and writing

1. What are the possible bases that Quintilian recognizes? Give an illustration of each from today's world.

2. Although this discussion of bases is illustrated principally with examples from legal disputes, might the advice given in the selection be of value to those arguing nonlegal questions, deliberative questions, for example, as well? Explain.

3. How might one proceed in analyzing a case or controversy in order to determine its "basis," or central issue?

4. Construct an argumentative paper on a subject of your own choosing in which you organize your ideas around the three questions Quintilian enumerates here. Then evaluate the cogency of your argument.

notes on analyzing issues and beginning the discourse

RICHARD WHATELY

Whately's ELEMENTS OF RHETORIC, *one of the major nineteenth-century instructional texts in rhetoric, was first published in 1828, then revised and enlarged several times. The book is directed primarily toward prospective preachers (Whately was Archbishop of Dublin), but its discussions of the selection and arrangement of arguments offer suggestions to writers and speakers on other subjects as well. The selection that follows, from "Of Introductions and Conclusions," describes some techniques for beginning a discourse. The discussion of "burden of proof" is thought to be one of Whately's most important contributions to the theory of rhetorical invention.*

1ST. One of the objects most frequently proposed in an Introduction, is, to show that the subject in question is *important, curious,* or otherwise *interesting,* and worthy of attention. This may be called an "Introduction inquisitive."

2ndly, It will frequently happen also, when the point to be proved or explained is one which may be very fully established, or on which there is little or no doubt, that it may nevertheless be *strange,* and different from what might have been expected; in which case it will often have a good effect in rousing the attention, to set forth as strongly as possible this *paradoxical* character, and dwell on the seeming improbability of that which must, after all, be admitted. This may be called an "Introduction paradoxical." For instance:—"If you should see a flock of pigeons in a field of corn: and if (instead of each picking where and what it liked, taking just as much as it wanted, and no more) you should see ninety-nine of them gathering all they got into a heap; reserving nothing for themselves but the chaff and the refuse; keeping this heap for one, and that the weakest, perhaps worst, of the flock; sitting round, and looking on, all the winter, whilst this one was devouring, throwing about, and wasting it; and if a pigeon, more hardy or hungry than the rest, touched a grain of the hoard, all the others instantly flying upon it, and tearing it to pieces; if you should see this, you would see nothing more than what is every day practised and established among men. Among men, you see the ninety and nine toiling and scraping together a heap of superfluities for one, (and this one too, oftentimes the feeblest and worst of the whole set, a child, a woman, a madman, or a fool;) getting nothing for themselves all the while, but a little of the coarsest of the provision, which their own industry produces; looking quietly on,

FROM RICHARD WHATELY, *The Elements of Rhetoric,* ED. DOUGLAS EHNINGER (CARBONDALE, ILL.: SOUTHERN ILLINOIS UNIVERSITY PRESS, 1963), PP. 112–115, 170–172. REPRINTED BY PERMISSION OF THE PUBLISHER.

while they see the fruits of all their labour spent or spoiled; and if one of the number take or touch a particle of the hoard, the others joining against him, and hanging him for the theft.

"There must be some very important advantages to account for an institution, which, in the view of it above given, is so paradoxical and unnatural.

"The principal of these advantages are the following:" &c.

3rdly, What may be called an "Introduction corrective," is also in frequent use; viz. to show that the subject has been *neglected, misunderstood,* or *misrepresented* by others. This will, in many cases, remove a most formidable obstacle in the hearer's mind, the anticipation of triteness, if the subject be,—or may be supposed to be,—a hacknied one: and it may also serve to remove or loosen such prejudices as might be adverse to the favourable reception of our Arguments.

4thly, It will often happen also, that there may be need to explain some *peculiarity* in the mode of reasoning to be adopted; to guard against some possible *mistake* as to the object proposed; or to apologize for some *deficiency:* this may be called the "Introduction preparatory."

5thly, and lastly, in many cases there will be occasion for what may be called a "Narrative Introduction," to put the reader or hearer in possession of the outline of some transaction, or the description of some state of things, to which references and allusions are to be made in the course of the Composition. Thus, in Preaching, it is generally found advisable to detail, or at least briefly to sum up, a portion of Scripture-history, or a parable, when either of these is made the subject of a Sermon.

Two or more of the Introductions that have been mentioned are often combined; especially in the Preface to a work of any length.

And very often the Introduction will contain appeals to various passions and feelings in the hearers; especially a feeling of approbation towards the speaker, or of prejudice against an opponent who has preceded him: but this is, as Aristotle has remarked, not confined to Introductions.

The *Title* of a book is evidently of the character of an Introduction; being indeed sometimes the only one: so that what has been just said respecting Introductions, will, for the most part, be applicable to Titles.

It is a matter of considerable nicety to make

choice of a good Title; neither unattractive, nor yet so full of pretension as either to excite disgust, or lead to disappointment. It is also, in one respect, more important than the exordium of a *Speech;* because the Orator who has opened injudiciously will yet usually obtain a *hearing,* in the course of which he may recover the lost ground; while an ill-chosen Title may prevent a Book from being read at all. . . .

. . .

It is a point of great importance to decide in each case, at the outset, in your own mind, and clearly to point out to the hearer, as occasion may serve on which side the *Presumption* lies, and to which belongs the *Burden of Proof.* For though it may often be expedient to bring forward more proofs than can be fairly *demanded* of you, it is always desirable, when this is the case, that it should be *known,* and that the strength of the cause should be estimated accordingly.

According to the most correct use of the term, a "Presumption" in favour of any supposition, means, not (as has been sometimes erroneously imagined) a preponderance of probability in its favour, but, such a *pre-occupation* of the ground, as implies that it must stand good till some sufficient reason is adduced against it; in short, that the *Burden of proof* lies on the side of him who would dispute it.

Thus, it is a well-known principle of the Law, that every man (including a prisoner brought up for trial) is to be *presumed* innocent till his guilt is established. This does not, of course, mean that we are to *take for granted* he is innocent; for if that were the case, he would be entitled to immediate liberation: nor does it mean that it is antecedently *more likely than not* that he is innocent; or, that the majority of these brought to trial are so. It evidently means only that the "burden of proof" lies with the accusers;—that he is not to be called on to prove his innocence, or to be dealt with as a criminal till he has done so; but that they are to bring their charges against him, which if he can repel, he stands acquitted.

Thus, again, there is a "presumption" in favour of the right of any individuals or bodies-corporate to the property of which they are in *actual possession.* This does not mean that they are, or are not, *likely* to be the rightful owners: but merely, that no man is to be disturbed in his possessions till some claim against him shall be established. He is not to be called on to prove his right; but the claimant, to disprove it; on whom consequently the "burden of proof" lies.

A moderate portion of common-sense will enable any one to perceive, and to show, on which side the Presumption lies, when once his attention is called to this question; though, for want of attention, it is often overlooked: and on the determination of this question the whole character of a discussion will often very much depend. A body of troops may be perfectly adequate to the defence of a fortress against any attack that may be made on it; and yet, if, ignorant of the advantage they possess, they sally forth into the open field to encounter the enemy, they may suffer a repulse. At any rate, even if strong enough to act on the offensive, they ought still to keep possession of their fortress. In like manner, if you have the "Presumption" on your side, and can but *refute* all the arguments brought against you, you have, for the present at least, gained a victory: but if you abandon this position, by suffering this Presumption to be forgotten, which is in fact *leaving out one of, perhaps, your strongest arguments,* you may appear to be making a feeble attack, instead of a triumphant defense.

Such an obvious case as one of those just stated, will serve to illustrate this principle. Let any one imagine a perfectly unsupported accusation of some offence to be brought against himself; and then let him imagine himself—instead of replying (as of course he would do) by a simple denial, and a defiance of his accuser to prove the charge,—setting himself to establish a negative,—taking on himself the burden of proving his own innocence, by collecting all the circumstances indicative of it that he can muster: and the result would be, in many cases, that this evidence would fall far short of establishing a certainty, and might even have the effect of raising a suspicion against him; he having in fact kept out of sight the important circumstance, that these probabilities in one scale, though of no great weight perhaps in themselves, are to be weighed against absolutely nothing in the other scale.

suggestions for discussion and writing

1. Examine a group of contemporary essays. Do the authors of these essays use the kinds of introductions Whately names? Give examples.

2. What kinds of introductions not listed by Whately do you find in contemporary writing and speaking?

3. In your own writing, do you use introductions similar to those described by Whately? If not, do you think your own essays might profit from an effort to use one or more of these introductions, as appropriate?

4. Write a group of short essays in which you use at least once each of the kinds of introduction Whately names.

5. In what kinds of issues (other than legal disputes) might it be wise for the writer to follow Whately's advice and discover where the "burden of proof" falls? Give some examples.

6. What are some techniques that one might use for discovering, in any issue, where the "burden of proof" falls? Apply these techniques in the planning of an argument on an issue of your own choosing.

The volume from which this extract is taken is a college text on rhetoric. Its special value lies in the authors' careful examination of how different rhetorical procedures help to give order to a subject and help to assure that the writer will communicate fully and precisely with his reader. The selection below, which is followed by a listing of kinds of definitions (omitted here because of space limitations), details some of the occasions when a writer may wish to use definition, and for what purposes. Dr. Martin, formerly head of freshmen English at Harvard, is now president of Union College. Dr. Ohmann formerly taught freshman English at Harvard and was later a Junior Fellow of the Society of Fellows. He is now on the faculty of Wesleyan University and is editor of COLLEGE ENGLISH.

the
uses
of
definition

HAROLD C. MARTIN AND
RICHARD M. OHMANN

WILLIAM James, the American psychologist and philosopher, once described an argument between two groups of people on a camping trip. Here is the problem they debated: a man is standing a few yards from a tree, and part way up the trunk, on the other side from the man, is a squirrel. The man moves around the tree trying to see the squirrel, but the squirrel keeps moving around the trunk, staying just opposite the man. Clearly the man goes around the tree, but does he go around the squirrel? One group said yes, one said no, both were equally convinced, and the argument, like the man and the squirrel, progressed in circles. James pointed out that the disagreement was not factual, but verbal. If "to go around something" means to progress in a circle around it, regardless of what *it* does in the middle, then the man does go around the squirrel. But if "to go around something" means to move from the front of it, to one side, to the back, to the other side, and finally to the front again, then the man does not go around the squirrel. Not all James's friends were content, but it seems clear that James had attacked the problem in the best possible way. If he did not "solve" it, in the sense of proving one side right, he at least *dissolved* the problem by showing that it was an unrewarding one unless couched in other terms. And of course he did so through definition.

The example is a trivial one, but the moral is not. Many puzzles of greater consequence create perplexity partly or entirely because of such confusions. Take for instance the old teaser as to whether a tree makes a sound if it falls in a deserted spot out of the hearing of man or animal. Or the still more ancient philosophical question about the

FROM HAROLD C. MARTIN AND RICHARD M. OHMANN, *The Logic and Rhetoric of Exposition*, REVISED EDITION (NEW YORK: HOLT, RINEHART AND WINSTON, INC., 1963), PP. 11–15. COPYRIGHT © 1957, 1958 BY HAROLD C. MARTIN. COPYRIGHT © 1963 BY HOLT, RINEHART AND WINSTON, INC. REPRINTED BY PERMISSION OF HOLT, RINEHART AND WINSTON, INC.

reality or unreality of objects. Instances abound in more practical matters, too. Are viruses alive? That depends partly on the definition of "alive." Is Algeria entitled to independence? Any discussion of the issue must include a definition of political rights. Is such and such a law unconstitutional? The answer may hinge partly on the meaning of "unconstitutional," and it will almost certainly depend upon the definition of words in the Constitution and in previous court opinions. Whenever the facts are certain but the controversy still lumbers on unfruitfully, it is wise to take a fresh look at the key terms of the controversy and at their meanings. Students and others who like firm answers may weary of the rejoinder, "It's all a matter of definition." And indeed, the call for definition can be tedious, question-begging, and sophistical: not every dilemma will be resolved by a clarification of terms. But clarity of terms is essential to every important argument, and definition offers a powerful means of brushing away intellectual cobwebs.

Many questions, like those in the preceding paragraph, cannot even be intelligently posed without definition. Hopeless to ask how much poverty there is in the United States unless there is some acceptable definition of poverty. Especially in problems of classification, definition is a prerequisite. Thus, in deciding which organizations were subversive, the Attorney General's office first had to define "subversive," implicitly or explicitly (it defined the word too loosely, to many people's taste). A well-known House committee decides at intervals whether certain activities are "un-American." The censors, and sometimes the courts, are asked to determine what books and movies are "obscene" or "blasphemous." As these decisions have serious practical consequences, so do the definitions they incorporate. Meteorologists cannot say how many *hurricanes* there were last year without definition; nor can critics decide when the *novel* arose as a literary form; nor teachers which students have done *satisfactory* work; nor the man on the street whether what he is about to do is *wrong*. Problems of all sorts, including many that students write about, are likely to become manageable only after a certain amount of defining.

Dilemmas, questions, and problems of classification often call for definition as a means to an end; some difficulties faced by the writer call for definition as an end in itself. Perhaps he is uneasy about the popular use of a certain word—as the

architect Richard Neutra was about the verb "own." Neutra thought it absurd to speak of a man as owning a house that was built, not for his individual needs, but to the specifications of a mass-produced stereotype, a house with no privacy in a row of identical houses, a house with a thirty-five-year mortgage. Ownership should imply more psychological control and more personal involvement than that, he argued. His problem was specifically one of definition, or rather of redefinition.

Similarly, a writer may wish to propose a new definition of a term in common use, even though the conventional definition is not so much wrong as incomplete or puzzling. This happens often in science: in a sense, men knew for a long time what electricity was, but scientists could not rest content with the layman's definition. In humbler pursuits, too, conceptual reform often comes with redefinition. There was a revolution in social work and penal practices when theorists began to think of a criminal not as an inherently bad man, but as the product of his environment. And definitions of education continue to proliferate, though everyone knows what education is, after a fashion. To define such terms is to attack conceptual and practical matters at their center.

Now and then the writer encounters a phenomenon, a complex of events, a way of behaving or thinking, which has persisted for some time and been vaguely noticed, but which has never been isolated, fenced in, and given a label. If he wishes to concentrate his attention on such a phenomenon, to analyze it, and to understand it, he will save a great deal of inconvenience and verbosity by *naming* it. There have always, no doubt, been people who washed their hands every ten minutes, or couldn't stop chewing their nails, or just had to touch every other lamp post, but the psychologist who gathered such quirks and oddities together under the heading "compulsive" did a service to his colleagues and to users of the language generally by providing a shorthand term and a definition. And innovation of this sort can often be much more than a procedural shortcut. Freud, by coining and applying "repression," the "Oedipus complex," the "id," the "death wish," and many others, opened the door on a whole new way of understanding the human mind, though the patterns of behavior referred to by his neologisms were probably as ancient as the family. To name and define is to reinterpret, as well as to reduce complexity.

Sometimes, too, naming and defining are ways

of overcoming newness and strangeness. History sometimes repeats itself. But it also dazzles the observer with novel arrangements of people and institutions, which only become "thinkable" as names and definitions are minted and pass into currency. "Cold war," "iron curtain," "balance of terror"—terms like these, though they sometimes lead to oversimplification, have helped postwar Americans to orient themselves within the turmoil of move and countermove brought on by the rise to power of Soviet Russia and the development of atomic weapons. Similarly, an obscure social upheaval assumed new clarity and shape for outsiders when Jack Kerouac labeled and defined the "beat generation." (In fact, one doubts that the movement itself would have flourished so healthily without the rallying point of a title.) The chance to make the new familiar through language does not present itself only to public men and novelists; even a student grappling with an assigned theme is likely to find that some obstacles melt away if he confronts them with name and definition.

The need for defining may also arise, not from the encounter with experience, but from the necessity of making words behave properly. Perhaps the writer wishes to introduce a technical term, say "entropy," one with which his readers may be unfamiliar. Clearly, if the word is to perform its function for him, he must define it before he proceeds. Or perhaps he wants to restrict the meaning of a common word to suit his purposes. It is within his rights, in an essay on traffic deaths, to use the word "accident" to mean "collision caused by a driver's carelessness or miscalculation" (thereby excluding murder, suicide, mechanical failure, etc.); but, if he takes this liberty with the word, he has an obligation to spell out for the reader just how much he has narrowed down the usual meaning, an obligation to define "stipulatively," as we shall call it. Again, it often happens that a writer imports a term from another field and uses it metaphorically or analogically in his own. Thus Matthew Arnold christened the English middle class "Philistines," and literary critics have come to speak of the "tension" in a poem between two attitudes, image clusters, patterns of structure, and so on. Since a metaphor or analogy never creates an exact equivalence, the writer who first takes such a leap must make it clear how much and how little of the original meaning he has carried along with him. These are procedures which will from time to time concern every writer except the most slavishly conventional; in bending language to one's special purposes it is often expedient to define.

Definition has a common use, too, in studies of other writers' thoughts. It would be difficult to describe the theme of Book I of *The Faerie Queene* without knowing what Spenser meant by "grace." Such concepts can be so central to the outlook of a man or an age that they deserve full-scale definition. Whole books have been devoted to the idea of progress, Shakespeare's concept of nature, the notion of romanticism, and so forth. In literary criticism, intellectual history, and philosophy, a great deal depends on understanding precisely how men have used their favorite terms, for the structures of human belief are accessible to the student only through scrutiny of the words men use to express those beliefs.

And (to make an end of this survey) defining serves the writer well even when he does it privately, never committing his definition to paper. For his very competence with language will be in part a consequence of adequate control over words and meanings. To say this is not simply to say that a writer should have a "big vocabulary." Although his vocabulary is immense, he may still confuse "infer" with "imply," or fail to understand the subtle distinction between "ethics" and "morality." He may commit stylistic blunders such as writing "this mistake and other ideas"—which he might avoid by simply defining "mistake" and "idea" for himself. He may overlook the difference in suggestiveness between "obedience" and "servility." And in general, his style will be flabby, wavering, and unpersuasive unless he is attuned to the intricacies of meaning that surround his words. Nor can his thought be lucid if it must wallow in vague and ambiguous language. The writer who protests, "You understood me, even if I didn't use the right word" is fooling himself and shirking the arduous job of writing plainly. Similarly, the writer who claims, "I know what I mean, but I can't put it into words" is mistaking a half-formed intuition for a fully explicit thought. Of course all writers, to one degree or another, possess a "feeling" for the words of their native languages; but even the most accomplished poet or novelist must frequently stop and ponder the appropriateness of this or that word. The neophyte will never grow as a writer without a constant effort to master the words he half-knows, and to study those with which he is barely acquainted: in short, a constant effort to define, if only for himself.

suggestions for discussion and writing

1. In the expository writing you have recently read, and in speeches you have heard, what examples of definition have you observed? Which of the purposes listed by Martin and Ohmann do these definitions illustrate?

2. On what additional occasions might explicit definition of terms be a valuable aid to ordering and clarifying discussion?

3. Martin and Ohmann assert that defining often helps a writer or speaker to clarify his own thoughts and improve his own diction even if in his writing and speaking he does not include formal definitions. Does your experience corroborate this assertion? Are there occasions when failure to define terms privately, for yourself, has weakened your powers of communication? Give examples.

4. Plan an essay that will serve one or more of the purposes listed by Martin and Ohmann. Write the major assertion that you will develop in the essay and determine what words in the assertion require definition. Then, write the essay.

5. Find some phenomenon or feature of behavior that puzzles or interests you and devise a name for it. Then write a definition of the term you have used as a name. After going through the process, do you agree that to name and define "is to reinterpret and reduce complexity"?

Dr. Gorrell is professor of English at the University of Nevada. He is coauthor of a major text on rhetoric and author of several articles on the theory of rhetoric. In 1964 he organized and chaired a national conference on new developments in the theory and teaching of the subject. In the passages that follow, Dr. Gorrell develops his theory of "commitment and response," which holds that every sentence generates in the reader expectations that the writer is obligated to fulfill, with the result that the options available to him as he writes his next sentences are limited. This theory is a fresh attempt to help writers solve their problems in designing and developing an essay.

the writer's commitment to his reader

ROBERT M. GORRELL

From "VERY LIKE A WHALE"

IT seems to me useful to make one approach to the sentence or paragraph—or any segment of discourse—as a sequence of commitments and responses. That is, when a writer selects a subject for his sentence or chooses a sentence opener, he commits himself to a limited number of patterns and a limited set of meanings that can follow. If what he wants to say about the subject, the predication which is probably his motive for making the statement, does not respond logically to the commitment he has made, he probably needs to start over. Or more broadly, a topic sentence or statement of a main idea can profitably be examined for more than its validity as a generalization, for the expectations it creates. Both the meaning and the structure of the statement make commitments, more or less restricting, which need to be honored. The topic sentence of a paragraph is likely to regulate the type of support that can follow, to determine something of the degrees of specificity which the development will attain, to help determine the organizational scheme of the paragraph. The following sentence rather obviously indicates what should follow it:

> The results of the efforts of these few grammarians may be illustrated by referring to a couple of pronouns and a few verbs.

The sentence limits the choices of the writer clearly; it is obviously framed to fit a preconceived plan for the paragraph. The responses must be examples using "a couple of pronouns and a few verbs." Another topic sentence is less limiting:

> Perhaps the most noticeable change that has occurred since 1500 is not in grammar but in vocabulary.

FROM "VERY LIKE A WHALE: A REPORT ON RHETORIC," *College Composition and Communication,* OCTOBER 1965, PP. 142–143, AND FROM "NOT BY NATURE: APPROACHES TO RHETORIC," *English Journal,* APRIL 1966, PP. 10–13. REPRINTED BY PERMISSION OF THE NATIONAL COUNCIL OF TEACHERS OF ENGLISH AND ROBERT M. GORRELL.

The writer has various choices for his next sentence, but he is also limited. He cannot start listing grammatical changes; he cannot turn to a generalization about the state of the language in 1500. He might mention a specific vocabulary change, he might make a general comment about vocabulary in 1500. Perhaps the most likely response is the one that does follow, a specification of the opening sentence:

> Through borrowings from dead Latin, dead Greek, and most of the important living languages of the world English has multiplied its store of words manyfold.

Such an approach to writing as a sequence of commitments and responses may have usefulness for rhetorical theory, may indicate something about how writing is generated; but it is more obviously a basis for practical exercises in paragraph construction, and it involves at the same time all stages in the composing process, from invention to the finished product.

From "NOT BY NATURE"

A second principle is that writing can be considered as continuity, as a series of commitments and responses. That is, the patterns which reveal the relationships of addition described above can also be looked at as a flow or a sequence.[1] Within the sentence, for instance, every predication or linkage pattern takes form partly because every word the writer chooses commits him in some way to what is to follow—limits him, sometimes quite narrowly, to the words—the responses—which may follow. When, for instance, the writer chooses a sentence subject, he commits himself in several ways to certain types of responses. If he chooses to begin with an abstraction like *his insistence* or *the reason,* he limits possibilities for following verbs. He eliminates action verbs like *jump* or *grumble;* he increases considerably the likelihood that his verb will be *is* or *was.* If he does select *is* or *was,* he is again committed, grammatically at least, to a modifier or subject complement as a response.

The principle is more significant, however, as an approach to longer units than sentences—as a way of looking at the development or generation of prose as a sequence of ideas. Consider the begin-

[1] In an earlier portion of the paper, Dr. Gorrell asserted that writing could be viewed as a process of adding comments to topics, and that the principal means of addition were predication, linkage, coordination, and subordination [Ed.].

ning of the paragraph above about words.[2] The opening sentence

> Some English words have a negative, but no positive.

makes a commitment; that is, it limits the possibilities that can follow. As a relatively general assertion, it creates an expectation in the reader; the reader expects in the following sentence to get further enlightenment about what the opening sentence means. The sentence commits the writer to saying more explicitly what he means—to illustrating, explaining, justifying, elaborating his opening assertion. Sentence 2 responds with a concrete, specific illustration, which clarifies the assertion of sentence 1. But sentence 2 also makes a commitment, and sentence 3 responds by citing another example. Sentence 4 responds to 3—and, of course, both 3 and 4 also respond to 1—with two more illustrations. One could go on through any segment of prose, analyzing various elements—words, sentences, parts of sentences, parts of paragraphs—as sequences of commitments and responses.

But I am interested in the concept less as a device for the analysis of existing prose than as a guide for the generation of prose—as a way of thinking about composition. The application of the principle to writing is obvious: every unit of composition must be conceived and tested both as a commitment to what follows and a response to what precedes. The implications of the principle are perhaps less obvious and are certainly far-reaching; they encompass much of practical rhetoric. They direct the writer—and of course the teacher of writing—to two basic considerations:

1 Commitment. Any unit of continuing prose makes a commitment, but it is convenient here to consider sentences. The writer must be aware of the kind of commitment each sentence makes. The opening sentence of the above paragraph might have been cast in many different ways, but any change would change the commitment. For example, the writers of the paragraph might have begun:

> Some English words offer variations which seem illogical and inconsistent.

The commitment here is much less restricting than in the original. The paragraph might go on to talk

[2] The paragraph in question appears at the end of this selection [Ed.].

about spelling variations, about unusual semantic changes—or about negatives without positives. The sentence offers less help than the original. If the sentence were still broader,

> Some English words present very interesting problems.

it would be almost useless as an opening for the paragraph, because it commits the writer so extensively that he can respond only in a book. On the other hand, a generalization as broad as this —though hopefully less vague and more meaningful—might serve usefully as an opening, making a commitment to several paragraphs or chapters. Because commitments vary in scope, a sentence may make a commitment to only the sentence following it, to three or four sentences—as does the opening sentence of the original—or to a whole book. If the writers had omitted the opening sentence, begun the paragraph with sentence 2, a different sort of problem would have existed: the opening sentence would have limited the possibilities of what could follow but would not have extended its influence so widely over the entire paragraph.

Such speculation about alternatives suggests obvious broad precepts, mostly variations on don't bite off more than you can chew, but bite off something. That is, at each stage in his composition the writer is making commitments—in form and in content. The commitment must not be so great that no sensible response is possible; a generalization must not include everything, but it must say something.

2 Response. Although obviously an unlimited number of specific sentences may follow any other, the types of likely responses to any commitment seem to me surprisingly few. In general, the writer seems to me committed to one of the following: *(a)* Specification, *(b)* Repetition, *(c)* Diversion.

(a) Specification. Probably the most common response to a commitment is an illustration, an example, an explanation. In the paragraph above, sentence 2 obviously responds to sentence 1 in this way. Or, in the following three sentences, William James moves to one level of increased specificity and then goes to examples:

> But, with all this beating and tacking on my part,
> I fear you take me to be reaching a confused result.

> I seem to be just taking things up and dropping them again.
> First I took up Chautauqua, and dropped that; then Tolstoi and the heroism of common toil, and dropped them; finally, I took up ideals, and seem now almost dropping those.

The Will To Believe and Other Essays (Reynolds, 1897).

The second sentence turns the paragraph to discussion of the first part of the first sentence, sharpening the focus. The third responds to the second with examples. In the following, the second sentence specifies somewhat differently.

> Because it is small, the small firm has one potential advantage over the big one. It can't afford big research teams to administrate or interlocking committees to work up programs, and it doesn't have a crystallized company "family" to adjust to.
> William H. Whyte, Jr.,
> *The Organization Man*
> (Simon and Shuster, 1956).

The first sentence asserts that the small firm has an advantage which is its very smallness. Then the second lists two or three specific aspects of this advantage of smallness.

Often the specification moves farther, selecting only part of a preceding sentence as its commitment and providing a specific emphasis for what is to follow. The second sentence of the paragraph above on words, for example, might have gone something like this:

> These words seldom cause difficulty, but they could provide temptations for anyone who likes to play games with words.

This kind of sentence would turn the generalization of the opening in a new direction, establishing a new kind of commitment. A third sentence, then, would have to be something like:

> They might stimulate someone to praise the convenience of *delible* ink, to come to an *evitable* conclusion, and to speak with *punity.*

The paragraph could go on, although it would be moving in a different way. The following illustrates the same sort of variation:

> If the essence of history is the memory of things said and done, then it is obvious that every normal

person, Mr. Everyman, knows some history. Of course we do what we can to conceal this invidious truth.

> Carl Becker,
> "Everyman His Own Historian,"
> *American Historical Review*
> (January, 1932).

The second sentence responds to only part of the assertion of the first, turning the direction enough that it might be considered a deviation as well as specification. As might be expected, the third sentence offers specification for sentence 2, for how we "conceal this invidious truth":

> Assuming a professional manner, we say that so and so knows no history, when we mean no more than that he failed to pass the examinations set for a higher degree; and simple-minded persons, undergraduates, and others, taken in by academic classifications of knowledge, think they know no history because they have never taken a course in history in college, or have never read Gibbon's *Decline and Fall of the Roman Empire*.

Interestingly, however, the paragraph after another sentence or two moves back to respond more directly to the opening sentence, providing specific support for the statement that Mr. Everyman knows some history.

(b) Repetition. It is also common to follow a sentence with another of the same sort, in effect paralleling or repeating a response to an earlier commitment. In the paragraph about words, sentence 3 responds to 2 by repeating on the same level of specificity adding a parallel example, and sentence 4 follows 3 in the same way. Or notice the sentence that follows those quoted above from William H. Whyte, Jr.:

> Because it hasn't caught up yet with modern management, to put it another way, it provides an absence of the controls that make the scientist restive.

The sentence may move slightly toward greater specificity than the one preceding it, but essentially it is a parallel, putting it another way.

(c) Deviation. Often a writer achieves movement of his ideas by using one sentence as the basis for a shift in a direction in a following one. That is, a possible response to a commitment may be a deviation, which turns the course of discourse, even reverses it. A possible second sentence for the

paragraph on words might have shifted direction:

> Most English negatives, however, have a corresponding positive.

Such a sentence would seem to commit the third to respond with examples of pairs: *intangible* and *tangible, invisible* and *visible,* and so on. Or, the second sentence might have gone even farther afield:

> This suggests that English speakers generally have taken a pessimistic view toward life.

Obviously, such a turn does not provide a very promising way to continue. A response which provides a deviation occurs most frequently along in the middle of a paragraph as a way of providing a kind of subtopic, as in the following:

> By temperament I lean to the side that considers composing in our community as a natural force —something to be taken for granted—rather than the freakish occupation of a very small minority of our citizens. And yet, judging the situation dispassionately, I can see that we ought not to take it for granted.
>
> > Aaron Copeland,
> > *Music and Imagination*
> > (Harvard University Press, 1952).

The paragraph continues with specification to develop the second sentence.

I have used examples of sentences in pairs to emphasize the continuity from sentence to sentence, but variations should be pointed out. Sometimes a response is made to an earlier commitment, as discourse breaks into units longer than a single sentence. In the paragraph above, for instance, sentence 5 is actually a response to the commitment of sentence 1, starting a new sequence in which 6 specifies 5, and the remaining sentences are parallel specifications of 6. On the other hand, a single sentence may present not only the commitment and response involved in the basic predication but also illustrative specification:

> Scholars have introduced learning spellings in many words,
> > e.g., *debt, doubt,* on account of Latin *debita, dubito,* formerly written as in French *dette, doute;*
> > *victuals,* formerly *vittles.*
> > > Otto Jespersen,
> > > *Essentials of English Grammar*
> > > (Allen and Unwin, 1933).

And, of course, responses do not necessarily fit neatly into the categories I have listed but frequently combine; a diversion often specifies, for example.

The paragraph analyzed on page 46 follows:

1 Some English words have a negative, but no positive. *2* Anything which is *indelible* cannot be erased, but there is no *delible*. *3* An *uncouth, unkempt* person is crude and untidy, but even if he should reform his ways, he would not be *couth* and *kempt*. *4* We can speak with *impunity,* but not with *punity,* be *immune* to disease, but not *mune*. *5* All these words, and others, were originally formed from a negative

prefix and a positive word. *6* In some cases the positive word was never taken into our language, but only the combined form with a negative meaning; in other cases the positive word eventually dropped out and only the negative combination remained. *7 Unkempt,* for instance, is from English *un-,* not, and *kempt,* a dialect form of *combed*. *8* We no longer use *kempt,* but have kept *unkempt* which from the original meaning of "uncombed" came to mean "generally untidy." *9 Indelible* is from Latin *in-,* not, and *delibilis,* perishable. *10* We adopted the Latin word *indelibilis*—but not delibilis—and changed it to *indelible*.

Helene and Charlton Laird,
The Tree of Language
(World, 1957)

suggestions for discussion and writing

1. What assumptions are made in these two essays about how a reader approaches and assimilates a piece of discourse?

2. In what ways, if any, does Gorrell depart from the emphases established by Aristotle, Cicero, and Quintilian in their discussions of how to organize and develop a discourse? In what ways does Gorrell continue the emphases of the three classical rhetoricians?

3. Take the opening sentence of an essay you have written recently (or write the opening sentence of what might be a new essay), and rewrite it in different words that say approximately the same thing as the first version. Have you changed the kind of commitment you made to your audience? How?

4. Analyze a few paragraphs from one or more professional essays to see whether you can identify the kinds of development about which Gorrell speaks.

Identify methods of developing a paragraph in addition to those listed by Gorrell.

5. In developing a piece of discourse, can a writer or speaker go beyond the commitments he has made to his reader or listener at the beginning? If he does, what problems does he face? How might he solve them?

6. Write a short essay in which you begin with an assertion and then deliberately try to discharge all of the commitments implied in that assertion. Evaluate the resulting essay. Do you still face problems in organizing the essay, or does the application of Gorrell's theory help you to eliminate most of your problems in organization?

7. In the section headed "From 'Not by Nature,'" what commitments does Gorrell make to his reader? Does he respond to these commitments satisfactorily in the rest of the piece? Explain your answer.

on style

QUINTILIAN

The last part of Quintilian's comprehensive textbook on rhetoric is primarily devoted to style. The selections that follow, from Books XI and XII, contain classic, if not original, statements about the value of decorum in style and about the three principal kinds of style. Quintilian insists, as did most Greek and Roman rhetoricians, that a speaker's style be adjusted to the audience and the occasion for speaking —a doctrine of which modern texts on rhetoric frequently remind us.

WHAT use is it if we employ a lofty tone in cases of trivial import, a slight and refined style in cases of great moment, a cheerful tone when our matter calls for sadness, a gentle tone when it demands vehemence, threatening language when supplication, and submissive when energy is required, or fierceness and violence when our theme is one that asks for charm? Such incongruities are as unbecoming as it is for men to wear necklaces and pearls and flowing raiment which are the natural adornments of women, or for women to robe themselves in the garb of triumph, than which there can be conceived no more majestic raiment. . . .

For this reason, it is of the first importance that we should know what style is most suitable for conciliating, instructing or moving the judge, and what effects we should aim at in different parts of our speech. Thus we shall eschew antique, metaphorical and newly-coined words in our *exordium, statement of facts* and *arguments,* as we shall avoid flowing periods woven with elaborate grace, when the case has to be divided and distinguished under its various heads, while, on the other hand, we shall not employ mean or colloquial language, devoid of all artistic structure, in the *peroration,* nor, when the theme calls for compassion, attempt to dry the tears of our audience with jests. For all ornament derives its effect not from its own qualities so much as from the circumstances in which it is applied, and the occasion chosen for saying anything is at least as important a consideration as what is actually said. . . .

. . .

There is another threefold division, whereby, it is held, we may differentiate three styles of speaking, all of them correct. The first is termed the plain, the second grand and forcible, and the third either intermediate or florid. The nature of these three styles is, broadly speaking, as follows. The first would seem best adapted for instructing, the second for moving, and the third (by whichever

FROM QUINTILIAN, *Institutio Oratoria,* TRANS. H. E. BUTLER (4 VOLS.; CAMBRIDGE, MASS.: HARVARD UNIVERSITY PRESS, 1958), IV, 155, 157—159, 483—487, 489. REPRINTED BY PERMISSION OF THE PUBLISHERS AND THE LOEB CLASSICAL LIBRARY.

name we call it) for charming or, as others would have it, conciliating the audience; for instruction the quality most needed is acumen, for conciliation gentleness, and for stirring the emotions force. Consequently it is mainly in the plain style that we shall state our facts and advance our proofs, though it should be borne in mind that this style will often be sufficiently full in itself without any assistance whatever from the other two. The intermediate style will have more frequent recourse to metaphor and will make a more attractive use of figures, while it will introduce alluring digressions, will be neat in rhythm and pleasing in its reflexions: its flow, however, will be gentle, like that of a river whose waters are clear, but overshadowed by the green banks on either side. But he whose eloquence is like to some great torrent that rolls down rocks and "disdains a bridge" and carves out its own banks for itself, will sweep the judge from his feet, struggle as he may, and force him to go whither he bears him. This is the orator that will call the dead to life (as, for example, Cicero calls upon Appius Caecus); it is in his pages that his native land itself will cry aloud and at times address the orator himself, as it addresses Cicero in the speech delivered against Catiline in the senate. Such an orator will also exalt his style by amplification and rise even to *hyper-*

bole, as when Cicero cries, "What Charybdis was ever so voracious!" or "By the god of truth, even Ocean's self," etc. (I choose these fine passages as being familiar to the student). It is such an one that will bring down the Gods to form part of his audience or even to speak with him, as in the following, "For on you I call, ye hills and groves of Alba, on you, I say, ye fallen altars of the Albans, altars that were once the peers and equals of the holy places of Rome." This is he that will inspire anger or pity, and while he speaks the judge will call upon the gods and weep, following him wherever he sweeps him from one emotion to another, and no longer asking merely for instruction. . . .

But eloquence cannot be confined even to these three forms of style. For just as the third style is intermediate between the grand and the plain style, so each of these three are separated by interspaces which are occupied by intermediate styles compounded of the two which lie on either side. For there are styles fuller or plainer than the plain, and gentler or more vehement than the vehement, while the gentler style itself may either rise to greater force or sink to milder tones. Thus we may discover almost countless species of styles, each differing from the other by some fine shade of difference.

suggestions for discussion and writing

1. What definition of "style" is implied in Quintilian's discussion of the subject?

2. What features of a writer's or speaker's language, in Quintilian's opinion, most noticeably create or influence his style?

3. What specific considerations, according to Quintilian, should guide a speaker or writer in his choice of style?

4. Using Quintilian's terms, how would you characterize the styles of some authors or speakers whose work

you have encountered recently. Illustrate your characterizations by giving examples from the work of these writers.

5. Are Quintilian's classifications of style of any value to writers or speakers today? Why or why not?

6. Prepare three essays all of which argue the same thesis. Write each essay in one of the three kinds of style mentioned by Quintilian, so that you have an example of each of his three styles. To what sort of audience might you present each of these essays?

*Semanticist, psychologist, philosopher, interpreter of
literature, and former University Professor at Harvard, I. A. Richards has published many influential
studies of language and literature, including* THE
MEANING OF MEANING *(with C. K. Ogden, 1923),*
PRINCIPLES OF LITERARY CRITICISM *(1924),* INTERPRE-
TATION IN TEACHING *(1938), and* SPECULATIVE IN-
STRUMENTS *(1955). Much of his work has dealt with
the processes of human communication and the
workings of words. In* THE PHILOSOPHY OF RHETORIC
*(1936), he dismisses as of virtually no value the
theories and teachings of many rhetoricians,
insisting that rhetoric ought to be a study of "misunderstanding and its remedies." His theory of rhetoric is based on his "context" theory of meaning,
which holds that a word acquires meaning by calling
to mind, not an object, but a context with which the
word is associated—"a whole cluster of events that
recur together" in a causal sequence. "What the . . .
word . . . means is the missing parts of the context"
(p. 34). In this selection—from Lecture III—Richards
works out some implications of this theory.*

the interinanimation of words

I. A. RICHARDS

I TURN now to that other sense of "context"—the
literary context—which I distinguished last
time from the technical sense of "context," as a
recurrent group of events, that is convenient for the
theorem of meaning. Let us consider some of the
effects on words of their combination in sentences,
and how their meaning depends upon the other
words before and after them in the sentence. What
happens when we try with a sentence to decide what
single words in it mean?

· · ·

The mutual dependence of words varies evidently with the type of discourse. At one end of the
scale, in the strict exposition of some highly criti-
cized and settled science through technicalized and
rigid speech, a large proportion of them are independent. They mean the same whatever other words
they are put with; or if a word fluctuates, it moves
only into a small number of stable positions, which
can be recorded and are anchored to definitions.
That is the ideal limit towards which we aim in
exposition. Unfortunately we tend—increasingly
since the Seventeenth Century—to take rigid
discourse as the norm, and impose its standards
upon the rest of speech. This is much as if we
thought that water, for all its virtues, in canals,
baths and turbines, were really a weak form of ice.
The other end of the scale is in poetry—in some
forms of poetry rather. We know very much less
about the behavior of words in these cases—when

their virtue is to have no fixed and settled meaning separable from those of the other words they occur with. There are many more possibilities here than the theory of language has yet tried to think out. Often the whole utterance in which the co-operating meanings of the component words hang on one another is not itself stable in meaning. It utters not one meaning but a *movement* among meanings. Of course, even in the strictest prose we always have one thing that may be described as a movement of meaning. We have change as the sentence develops. In "The cat is on the mat" we begin with the cat and end with the mat. There is a progression of some sort in every explicit sentence. But in the strictest prose the meanings of the separate words theoretically stay put and thought passes from one to another of them. At the other end of the scale the whole meaning of the sentence shifts, and with it any meanings we may try to ascribe to the individual words. In the extreme case it will go on moving as long as we bring fresh wits to study it. When Octavius Cæsar is gazing down at Cleopatra dead, he says,

> She looks like sleep,
> As she would catch another Antony
> In her strong toil of grace.

"Her strong toil of grace." Where, in terms of what entries in what possible dictionary, do the meanings here of *toil* and *grace* come to rest?

But my subject is Rhetoric rather than Poetics and I want to keep to prose which is not too far from the strict scientific or "rigid" end of this scale of dependent variabilities. In the kind of prose I am talking now, you have usually to wait till I have gone on a bit before you can decide how you will understand the opening parts of the sentences. If, instead, I were reading you the first few theorems of Euclid, that would not be so. You would understand, as soon as I said "a triangle," what the word meant, and though what I went on to say might qualify the meaning ("having two sides equal"), it would not destroy or completely change the meaning that you had so far given to the word. But in most prose, and more than we ordinarily suppose, the opening words have to wait for those that follow to settle what they shall mean—if indeed that ever gets settled.

All this holds good not only as to the *sense* of the waiting words but as regards all the other functions of language which we can distinguish and set over against the mere sense. It holds for the *feeling* if any towards what I am talking about, for *the relation towards my audience* I want to establish or maintain with the remark, and for the *confidence* I have in the soundness of the remark—to mention three main sorts of these other language functions. . . .

• • •

I have been leading up—or down, if you like—to an extremely simple and obvious but fundamental remark: that no word can be judged as to whether it is good or bad, correct or incorrect, beautiful or ugly, or anything else that matters to a writer, in isolation. That seems so evident that I am almost ashamed to say it, and yet it flies straight in the face of the only doctrine that for two hundred years has been officially inculcated—when any doctrine is inculcated in these matters. I mean the doctrine of Usage. The doctrine that there is a right or a good use for every word and that literary virtue consists in making that good use of it.

• • •

. . . I had better cite you a sentence or two in evidence, or you may think I am inventing a ghost to exorcize. I will take them from a *Manual of Rhetoric* which carries the names of three authors: Messrs. Gardiner, Kittredge and Arnold. . . . This is what they say of correctness: "Correctness is the most elementary of all requirements. The meanings of words are settled by usage. If we use a word incorrectly—that is in a sense which does not customarily belong to it—our readers will miss our thought, or, at best, they must arrive at it by inference and guesswork."

Inference and guesswork! What else is interpretation? How, apart from inference and skilled guesswork, can we be supposed ever to understand a writer or speaker's thought? This is, I think, a fine case of poking the fire from the top. But I have still my main bit of evidence to give you. My authors say: "In studying the four great principles of choice, we observe that only the first (correctness) involves the question of right and wrong. The others deal with questions of discrimination between better and worse—that is with the closer adaptation of words to the thoughts and feelings which we undertake to express. Further, it is only in dealing with the first principle (correctness) that we can keep our attention entirely on the single word."

There! that is the view I wished to illustrate. . . . The important point is that words are here supposed just sheerly to possess their sense, as men have their names in the reverse case, and to carry this meaning with them into sentences regardless of the neighbour words. That is the assumption I am attacking, because, if we follow up its practical consequences in writing and reading and trace its effects upon interpretation, we shall find among them no small proportion of the total of our verbal misunderstandings.

. . .

. . . Its evil is that it takes the senses of an author's words to be things we know before we read him, fixed factors with which he has to build up the meaning of his sentences as a mosaic is put together of discrete independent tesserae. Instead, they are resultants which we arrive at only through the interplay of the interpretative possibilities of the whole utterance. In brief, we have to guess them and we guess much better when we realize we are guessing, and watch out for indications, than when we think we know.

There are as many morals for the writer as for the reader in all this, but I will keep to interpretation. A word or phrase when isolated momentarily from its controlling neighbours is free to develop irrelevant senses which may then beguile half the other words to follow it. And this is at least equally true with the language functions *other than sense,* with *feeling,* say. I will give you one example of an erratic interpretation of feeling, and if I take it from the same *Manual of Rhetoric* that is because it illustrates one of the things to which the mosaic view or habit of interpretation, as opposed to the organic, often leads.

The Authors give the following from Bacon's *Advancement of Learning.* And in re-reading it I will ask you to note how cunningly Bacon, in describing some misuses of learning, takes back with one hand what he seems to be offering with the other, indicating both why men do prefer misuses and why they should not do so.

But the greatest error of all the rest is the mistaking or misplacing of the last or furthest end of knowledge. For men have entered into a desire of learning and knowledge, sometimes upon a natural curiosity and inquisitive appetite; sometimes to entertain their minds with variety and delight; sometimes for ornament and reputation; and sometimes to enable them to victory of wit and contradiction; and most times for lucre and profession; and seldom sincerely to give a true account of their gift of reason, to the benefit and use of men: as if there were sought in knowledge a couch, whereupon to rest a searching or restless spirit; or a terrace, for a wandering and variable mind to walk up and down with a fair prospect; or a tower of state, for a proud mind to raise itself upon; or a fort or commanding ground, for strife and contention; or a shop, for profit or sale; and not a rich storehouse, for the glory of the Creator and the relief of man's estate.

There is much to take to heart here—especially as to the couch aspect of the Usage Doctrine, and, I must admit, the tower and the fort—but what the authors say about it is this:

Here the splendor of the imagery is no mere embellishment. Without it, Bacon could not have given adequate expression to his enthusiastic appreciation of learning and his fine scorn for the unworthy uses to which it is sometimes put. At the same time, the figures elevate the passage from the ordinary levels of prose to a noble eloquence. (p. 372)

What splendor is there in the imagery? These images have no splendor as Bacon uses them, but are severely efficient, a compact means for saying what he has to say. His "enthusiastic appreciation" (a poor phrase, I suggest, to smudge over him!) of the use of knowledge and his "fine scorn" of unworthy uses are given only if we refuse to be beguiled by the possibilities of splendor in the isolated images. Loose them even a little from their service, let their "splendor" act independently, and they begin at once to fight against his intention. For the terrace, the tower and the fort, if they were allowed to "elevate," would make the misplacings of the last and furthest end of knowledge seem much grander than "a true account of their gift of reason, to the benefit and use of men"—as a terrace or tower of state or a fort will seem grander than a mere rich storehouse.

suggestions for discussion and writing

1. In literature, particularly poetry, why do single words exhibit a considerable movement among meanings?

2. What implications does Richards' theory have for the interpretation of a word—for an understanding of its meaning and its value in characterizing the speaker's "voice" and indicating his attitude toward his hearer?

3. What implications does the theory have for a doctrine of correctness or propriety, such as the doctrines Richards cites?

4. What responsibilities, according to Richards, must the reader or listener assume, if he is to understand words successfully?

5. What reponsibilities does a speaker or writer have to assume, if he accepts Richards' theories?

6. What implications does Richards' discussion have for a theory of the workings of metaphor? Find some passages from the work of professional writers in which the context controls, and perhaps enriches, the meanings of more or less familiar words. Find some passages in your own writing in which these effects occur. Change the word or words whose mean-ings you think are affected by their contexts, and explain what you have done to the way a reader might understand the passage.

7. Using a passage (of poetry, for example) in which one or more metaphors figure prominently, write an essay explaining the various meanings the metaphor(s) may have in context.

8. In an essay entitled "Ultimate Terms in Contemporary Rhetoric" (published in *The Ethics of Rhetoric,* 1957) Richard Weaver lists what he calls "god terms" and "devil terms" frequently used by contemporary writers. "God terms" ("progress," "science," "American," and so on) are words that automatically confer praise on the subject to which they are applied; "devil terms" ("Communist," "fascist," "prejudice," and so on) are words that automatically condemn the subject to which they are applied. (At least the terms have these effects in much popular writing.) Is the existence of these terms an example of "the interinanimation of words," or might their effects best be explained another way? Is the study of such "god terms" and "devil terms," in your opinion, a useful part of the study of "misunderstanding and its remedies"?

In this essay and in a companion essay entitled "A Generative Rhetoric of the Paragraph" (1965), Professor Christensen sets himself a task not often attempted before: to direct student writers in the production of sentences and paragraphs that resemble the sentences and paragraphs of professional writers. Hence the term "generative" in his titles; Professor Christensen hopes to describe techniques by which a writer can deliberately generate effective sentences and paragraphs. His essays are the fruit of extensive study of professional writing in the twentieth century, and he draws too on several years of experience as director of freshman English at the University of Southern California (from which he recently retired).

a generative rhetoric of the sentence

FRANCIS CHRISTENSEN

I F the new grammar is to be brought to bear on composition, it must be brought to bear on the rhetoric of the sentence. We have a workable and teachable, if not a definitive, modern grammar; but we do not have, despite several titles, a modern rhetoric.

. . .

The chapters on the sentence [in contemporary rhetorics] all appear to assume that we think naturally in primer sentences, progress naturally to compound sentences, and must be taught to combine the primer sentences into complex sentences— and that complex sentences are the mark of maturity. We need a rhetoric of the sentence that will do more than combine the ideas of primer sentences. We need one that will *generate* ideas.

For the foundation of such a generative or productive rhetoric I take the statement from John Erskine, the originator of the Great Books courses, himself a novelist. In an essay "The Craft of Writing" (*Twentieth Century English*, Philosophical Library, 1946) he discusses a principle of the writer's craft, which though known he says to all practitioners, he has never seen discussed in print. The principle is this: "When you write, you make a point, not by subtracting as though you sharpened a pencil, but by adding." We have all been told that the formula for good writing is the concrete noun and the active verb. Yet Erskine says, "What you say is found not in the noun but in what you add to qualify the noun . . . The noun, the verb, and the main clause serve merely as the base on which meaning will rise . . . The modifier is the essential part of any sentence." The foundation, then, for a generative or productive rhetoric of the sentence is that composition is essentially a process of *addition*.

But speech is linear, moving in time, and writ-

FROM *College Composition and Communication*, OCTOBER 1963, PP. 155–160. REPRINTED BY PERMISSION OF THE NATIONAL COUNCIL OF TEACHERS OF ENGLISH AND FRANCIS CHRISTENSEN.

ing moves in linear space, which is analogous to time. When you add a modifier, whether to the noun, the verb, or the main clause, you must add it either before the head or after it. If you add it before the head, the direction of modification can be indicated by an arrow pointing forward; if you add it after, by an arrow pointing backward. Thus we have the second principle of a generative rhetoric —the principle of *direction of modification* or *direction of movement*.

Within the clause there is not much scope for operating with this principle. The positions of the various sorts of close, or restrictive, modifiers are generally fixed and the modifiers are often obligatory—"The man who came to dinner remained till midnight." Often the only choice is whether to add modifiers. What I have seen of attempts to bring structural grammar to bear on composition usually boils down to the injunction to "load the patterns." Thus "pattern practice" sets students to accreting sentences like this: "The small boy on the red bicycle who lives with his happy parents on our shady street often coasts down the steep street until he comes to the city park." This will never do. It has no rhythm and hence no life; it is tone-deaf. It is the seed that will burgeon into gobbledygook. One of the hardest things in writing is to keep the noun clusters and verb clusters short.

It is with modifiers added to the clause—that is, with sentence modifiers—that the principle comes into full play. The typical sentence of modern English, the kind we can best spend our efforts trying to teach, is what we may call the *cumulative sentence*. The main clause, which may or may not have a sentence modifier before it, advances the discussion; but the additions move backward, as in this clause, to modify the statement of the main clause or more often to explicate or exemplify it, so that the sentence has a flowing and ebbing movement, advancing to a new position and then pausing to consolidate it, leaping and lingering as the popular ballad does. The first part of the preceding compound sentence has one addition, placed within it; the second part has 4 words in the main clause and 49 in the five additions placed after it.

The cumulative sentence is the opposite of the periodic sentence. It does not represent the idea as conceived, pondered over, reshaped, packaged, and delivered cold. It is dynamic rather than static, representing the mind thinking. The main clause ("the additions move backward" above) exhausts

the mere fact of the idea; logically, there is nothing more to say. The additions stay with the same idea, probing its bearings and implications, exemplifying it or seeking an analogy or metaphor for it, or reducing it to details. Thus the mere form of the sentence generates ideas. It serves the needs of both the writer and the reader, the writer by compelling him to examine his thought, the reader by letting him into the writer's thought.

Addition and direction of movement are structural principles. They involve the grammatical character of the sentence. Before going on to other principles, I must say a word about the best grammar as the foundation for rhetoric. I cannot conceive any useful transactions between teacher and students unless they have in common a language for talking about sentences. The best grammar is the grammar that best displays the layers of structure of the English sentence. The best I have found in a textbook is the combination of immediate constituent and transformation grammar in Paul Roberts's *English Sentences*. Traditional grammar, whether over-simple as in the school tradition or over-complex as in the scholarly tradition, does not reveal the language as it operates; it leaves everything, to borrow a phrase from Wordsworth, "in disconnection dead and spiritless." *English Sentences* is oversimplified and it has gaps, but it displays admirably the structures that rhetoric must work with—primarily sentence modifiers, including relative and subordinate clauses, but, far more important, the array of noun, verb, and adjective clusters. It is paradoxical that Professor Roberts, who has done so much to make the teaching of composition possible, should himself be one of those who think that it cannot be taught. Unlike Ulysses, he doesn't see any work for Telemachus to work.

Layers of structure, as I have said, is a grammatical concept. To bring in the dimension of meaning, we need a third principle—that of *levels of generality* or *levels of abstraction*. The main clause is likely to be stated in general or abstract or plural terms. With the main clause stated, the forward movement of the sentence stops, the writer shifts down to a lower level of generality or abstraction or to singular terms, and goes back over the same ground at this lower level.[1] "He has just

[1] Cf. Leo Rockas, "Abstract and Concrete Sentences," CCC, May 1963. Rockas describes sentences as abstract or concrete, the abstract implying the concrete and vice versa. Readers and writers, he says, must have the knack

bought a new car, a 1963½ Ford, a Galaxie, a fastback hardtop with four-on-the-floor shift." There is no theoretical limit to the number of structural layers or levels, each at a lower level of generality, any or all of them compounded, that a speaker or writer may use. For a speaker, listen to Lowell Thomas; for a writer, study William Faulkner. To a single independent clause he may append a page of additions, but usually all clear, all grammatical, once we have learned how to read him. Or, if you prefer, study Hemingway, the master of the simple sentence: "George was coming down in the telemark position, kneeling, one leg forward and bent, the other trailing, his sticks hanging like some insect's thin legs, kicking up puffs of snow, and finally the whole kneeling, trailing figure coming around in a beautiful right curve, crouching, the legs shot forward and back, the body leaning out against the swing, the sticks accenting the curve like points of light, all in a wild cloud of snow."

This brings me to the fourth, and last, principle, that of texture. *Texture* provides a descriptive or evaluative term. If a writer adds to few of his nouns or verbs or main clauses and adds little, the texture may be said to be thin. The style will be plain or bare. The writing of most of our students is thin—even threadbare. But if he adds frequently or much or both, then the texture may be said to be dense or rich. One of the marks of an effective style, especially in narrative, is variety in the texture, the texture varying with the change in pace, the variation in texture producing the change in pace. It is not true, as I have seen it asserted, that fast action calls for short sentences; the action is fast in the sentence by Hemingway above. In our classes, we have to work for greater density and variety in texture and greater concreteness and particularity in what is added.

I have been operating at a fairly high level of generality. Now I must downshift and go over the same points with examples. The most graphic way to exhibit the layers of structure is to indent the word groups of a sentence and to number the levels. Since in the narrow columns of this journal indentation is possible only with short sentences whose

additions are short, I have used it with only the first three sentences; the reader is urged to copy out the others for himself. I have added symbols to mark the grammatical character of the additions: SC, subordinate clause; RC, relative clause; NC, noun cluster; VC, verb cluster; AC, adjective cluster; Abs, absolute (i.e., a VC with a subject of its own); PP, prepositional phrase. With only a few exceptions (in some the punctuation may be questioned) the elements set off as on a lower level are marked by junctures or punctuation. The examples have been chosen to illustrate the range of constructions used in the lower levels; after the first few they are arranged by the number of levels. The examples could have been drawn from poetry as well as from prose. Those not attributed are by students.

1

1 He shook his hands,
  2 a quick shake, (NC)
    3 fingers down, (Abs)
      4 like a pianist. (PP)—Sinclair Lewis

2

  2 Calico-coated, (AC)
  2 small bodied, (AC)
  2 with delicate legs and pink faces (PP)
    3 in which their mismatched eyes rolled wild and subdued, (RC)
1 they huddled,
  2 gaudy motionless and alert, (AC)
  2 wild as deer, (AC)
  2 deadly as rattlesnakes, (AC)
  2 quiet as doves. (AC)—William Faulkner

3

1 The bird's eye, / , remained fixed upon him;
  2 bright and silly as a sequin (AC)
1 its little bones, / , seemed swooning in his hand.
  2 wrapped . . . in a warm padding of feathers (VC) —Stella Benson

4

(1) The jockeys sat bowed and relaxed, moving a little at the waist with the movement of their horses[2-VC].—Katherine Anne Porter

5

(1) The flame sidled up the match, driving a film of moisture and a thin strip of darker grey before it[2-VC].

---

of apprehending the concrete in the abstract and the abstract in the concrete. This is true and valuable. I am saying that within a single sentence the writer may present more than one level of generality, translating the abstract into the more concrete in added levels.

6

(1) She came among them behind the man, gaunt in the gray shapeless garment and the sunbonnet$^{2\text{-AC}}$, wearing stained canvas gymnasium shoes$^{2\text{-VC}}$. —Faulkner

7

(1) The Texan turned to the nearest gatepost and climbed to the top of it, his alternate thighs thick and bulging in the tight jeans$^{2\text{-Abs}}$, the butt of his pistol catching and losing the sun in pearly gleams$^{2\text{-Abs}}$.—Faulkner

8

(1) He could sail for hours, searching the blanched grasses below him with his telescopic eyes$^{2\text{-VC}}$, gaining height against the wind$^{2\text{-VC}}$, descending in mile-long, gently declining swoops when he curved and rode back$^{2\text{-VC}}$, never beating a wing$^{2\text{-VC}}$.—Walter Van Tilburg Clark

9

(1) The gay-sweatered skaters are quick-silvering around the frosty rink, the girls gliding and spinning$^{2\text{-Abs}}$, the boys swooping and darting$^{2\text{-Abs}}$, their arms flailing like wings$^{3\text{-Abs}}$.

10

(1) He stood at the top of the stairs and watched me, I waiting for him to call me up$^{2\text{-Abs}}$, he hesitating to come down$^{2\text{-Abs}}$, his lips nervous with the suggestion of a smile$^{3\text{-Abs}}$, mine asking whether the smile meant come, or go away$^{3\text{-Abs}}$

11

(1) Joad's lips stretched tight over his long teeth for a moment, and (1) he licked his lips, like a dog$^{2\text{-PP}}$, two licks$^{3\text{-NC}}$, one in each direction from the middle$^{4\text{-NC}}$.—Steinbeck

12

(1) We all live in two realities: one of seeming fixity$^{2\text{-NC}}$, with institutions, dogmas, rules of punctuation, and routines$^{3\text{-PP}}$, the calendared and clockwise world of all but futile round on round$^{4\text{-NC}}$; and one of whirling and flying electrons, dreams, and possibilities$^{2\text{-NC}}$, behind the clock$^{3\text{-PP}}$.—Sidney Cox

13

(1) It was as though someone, somewhere, had touched a lever and shifted gears, and (1) the hospital was set for night running, smooth and silent$^{2\text{-AC}}$, its normal clatter and hum muffled$^{2\text{-Abs}}$, the only sounds heard in the whitewalled room distant and unreal$^{2\text{-Abs}}$: a low hum of voices from the nurse's desk$^{3\text{-NC}}$, quickly stifled$^{4\text{-VC}}$, the soft squish of rubber-soled shoes on the tiled corridor$^{3\text{-NC}}$, starched white cloth rustling against itself$^{3\text{-NC}}$, and outside, the lonesome whine of wind in the country night$^{3\text{-NC}}$, and the Kansas dust beating against the windows$^{3\text{-NC}}$.

14

(1) The beach sounds are Jazzy, percussion fixing the mode$^{2\text{-Abs}}$—the surf cracking and booming in the distance$^{3\text{-Abs}}$, a little nearer dropped bar-bells clanking$^{3\text{-Abs}}$, steel gym rings, flung together$^{4\text{-VC}}$, ringing$^{3\text{-Abs}}$, palm fronds rustling above me$^{3\text{-Abs}}$, like steel brushes washing over a snare drum$^{4\text{-PP}}$, troupes of sandals splatting and shuffling on the sandy cement$^{3\text{-Abs}}$, their beat varying$^{4\text{-Abs}}$, syncopation emerging and disappearing with changing paces$^{5\text{-Abs}}$.

15

(1) A small negro girl develops from the sheet of glare-frosted walk, walking barefooted$^{2\text{-VC}}$, her bare legs striking and coiling from the hot cement$^{3\text{-Abs}}$, her feet curling in$^{4\text{-Abs}}$, only the outer edges touching$^{5\text{-Abs}}$.

16

(1) The swells moved rhythmically toward us irregularly faceted$^{2\text{-VC}}$, sparkling$^{2\text{-VC}}$, growing taller and more powerful$^{2\text{-VC}}$, until the shining crest bursts$^{3\text{-SC}}$, a transparent sheet of pale green water spilling over the top$^{4\text{-Abs}}$, breaking into blue-white foam as it cascades down the front of the wave$^{5\text{-VC}}$, piling up in a frothy mound that the diminishing wave pushes up against the pilings$^{5\text{-VC}}$, with a swishmash$^{6\text{-PP}}$, the foam drifting back $^{5\text{-Abs}}$, like a lace fan opened over the shimmering water as the spent wave returns whispering to the sea$^{6\text{-PP}}$.

The best starting point for a composition unit based on these four principles is with two-level narrative sentences, first with one second-level addition (sentences *4, 5*), then with two or more parallel ones (*6, 7, 8*). Anyone sitting in his room with his eyes closed could write the main clause of most of the examples; the discipline comes with the additions, provided they are based at first on immediate observation, requiring the student to phrase an exact observation in exact language. This can hardly fail to be exciting to a class: it is life, with the variety and complexity of life; the workbook exercise is death. The situation is ideal also for teaching diction—abstract-concrete, general-specific, literal-metaphorical, denotative-connotative. When the sentences begin to come out right, it is time to examine the additions for their grammatical character. From then on the grammar comes to the aid of the writing and the writing reinforces the grammar. One can soon go on to multi-level narrative sentences (*1, 3, 9–11, 15, 16*) and then to brief narratives of three to six or seven sentences on actions that can be observed over and over again—beating eggs, making a cut with a power saw, or following a record changer's cycle or a wave's flow and ebb. Bring the record changer to class. Description, by contrast, is static, picturing appearance rather than behavior. The constructions to master are the noun and adjective clusters and the absolute (*13, 14*). Then the descriptive noun cluster must be taught to ride piggy-back on the narrative sentence, so that description and narration are interleaved: "In the morning we went out into a new world, a glistening crystal and white world, each skeleton tree, each leafless brush, even the heavy, drooping power lines sheathed in icy crystal." The next step is to develop the sense for variety in texture and change in pace that all good narrative demands.

In the next unit, the same four principles can be applied to the expository paragraph. But this is a subject for another paper.

suggestions for discussion and writing

1. Give a definition of the "cumulative sentence" in your own words.

2. What qualities of sentences does Professor Christensen seem especially to seek or value? What qualities does he try to help writers avoid? Do you share his preferences? If not, why not? What kind of style do *you* value?

3. What benefits do you think might come to a writer who deliberately follows Christensen's advice about ways of generating sentences? To what dangers, if any, do you think a writer following Christensen's suggestions might fall prey?

4. Would other commentators on style in this collection approve or disapprove of Christensen's advice, or can you not tell what their opinions of his essay might be? Explain your position.

5. Professor Christensen says that his four principles can be applied to expository paragraphs. Before trying out the principles on one or more expository paragraphs, test them on sentences drawn from expository essays. Do the sentences you have chosen exhibit these principles? Would they have been more effective if they had exhibited these principles?

6. Write a sentence of description that might be developed in two or three paragraphs; the sentence should contain subject, verb, and object, or subject, verb, and complement. Then add modifiers (including participial and absolute constructions, if possible) to make the sentence more concrete and particular than before addition. Test the sentence (with additions) to see whether you have achieved the goals Christensen suggests for the generating of sentences.

7. Write one sentence summarizing Christensen's essay (or any other article in this volume). Use modifiers before the subject and after the verb or complement, so that you can include in the sentence Christensen's subordinate as well as his primary ideas. Then evaluate the clarity and usefulness of your sentence for one who has not read the essay.

Professor of English at the University of California, Berkeley, and a well-known poet, Josephine Miles has studied extensively the rhetorical and linguistic techniques of major English and American prose writers. The notes to her anthology, CLASSIC ESSAYS IN ENGLISH *(Revised Edition), contain numerous suggestions about the analysis of prose from the early sixteenth century to the present day. This essay seeks to apply grammatical concepts to the precise analysis of prose style and to suggest how the study of style and grammar can help students in the designing of essays and in the making of syntactic choices.*

what we compose

JOSEPHINE MILES

WHEN I looked at a passage of prose one day, I recognized a structural pattern in it, and when I tested my sense of this pattern, in a number of different writers, I found three or four major variations which served to suggest its relevance and pervasiveness. My specific method was to combine analysis of the frequencies of the main parts of speech in an eight thousand word prose text with a structural analysis of representative passages from the text.

The basic fact for observation is the tripartite articulation of utterance in formal prose: that is, first, the nucleus of predicated subject; second, the specification of context by adjectival and substantive modification, and third, the arrangement or composition by order and explicit connection. Thus the three main function-classes, each with its substitutable forms, are assertion (subject-predicate), development (modifying words), and connection (prepositional, conjunctival terms introducing phrasal and clausal structures). Like a word, with its root and specifying affixes and connecting affixes, a sentence specifies and relates its nucleus of assertion; and like a sentence, an essay or formal prose passage also asserts, develops, and relates. The sentence then may well provide, over a span of recurrences, a microcosm for the choices of distribution and emphasis in the statement as a whole; and thus a style, a regularity of distribution of sentence-elements, an habitual set of choices and emphases from sentence to sentence, may be discriminable in certain main types in English prose.

. . .

One of the great insights into grammar is, I think, that not content alone, but also context, defines the working units; that both character and location are part of their definition. Thus we may see that the basic parts of speech, substantive, predicate, modifier, and connective, are not just items but are also functions, and perhaps any of the items

FROM *College Composition and Communication,* OCTOBER 1963, PP. 147–154. REPRINTED BY PERMISSION OF THE NATIONAL COUNCIL OF TEACHERS OF ENGLISH AND JOSEPHINE MILES.

may serve any of the functions interchangeably, and word-order may be as vital to meaning as word-form. So too with sentences. The root of the sentence has its affixes, that is, time—place—manner—modifiers, as does the root of the word; and the sentence like the word is not an independent unit, a free form, because its meaning is dependent upon order as well as on content. The order of "He did not sing. He wanted to sing," makes a meaning different from "He wanted to sing. He did not sing." Even more, the use of connectives rests upon order. "He did not sing. But he wanted to sing" is normally more meaningful than "But he wanted to sing. He did not sing." Content and context thus are accentable by the connective signals. In composition, the selection of material is supported and conditioned by the ordering of the material, its *position,* and by the devices of signaling order, the connectives, which make up a large part of the *com*—in *composition*—the signs which put the idea together, and put us together with it.

One of the simplest ways to observe and follow significant order, then, is to pay close attention to the connectives in a passage—to note not only whether the idea moves by words, phrases, or clauses, but also by which sort it moves—by additives like *and, then, also,* by comparatives like *as, so, how,* by disjunctives like *but,* by alternatives like *on the one hand . . . on the other,* by causal subordinates like *if, because, for,* by descriptive subordinates like *who* and *which,* by temporal and spatial locatives like *where* and *there, when* and *then.* Behind these guiding signs lie three or four basic logical patterns of which we profoundly need to be aware.

The major word-connectives we use today had their sources in other forms, in other parts of speech. *And* was *ante* or *anti*—two parties face to face across a border, one and the other. *But,* on the other hand, excluded, made an exception of the other party. *Because* was the phrase *by cause.* Most conjunctions, adverbs, and prepositions are signs of spatial, temporal, and conceptual relations, of separating and joining, preceding and following.

Let us look at their procedures in some vigorous and distinguished prose styles: for example, that of Emerson near the beginning of *Self-Reliance.* The subject-predicate units are italicized, in contrast to the modifiers.

Travelling is a fool's *paradise.* Our first *journeys discover* to us the *indifference* of places.

At home *I dream that* at Naples, at Rome, *I can be intoxicated* with beauty *and lose my sadness. I pack my trunk, embrace my friends, embark* on the sea, *and* at last *wake up* in Naples, *and there* beside me *is the* stern *fact, the* sad *self,* unrelenting, identical, that I fled from. *I seek the Vatican and palaces. I affect to be intoxicated* with sights and suggestions, *but I am not intoxicated. My giant goes* with me wherever I go.

But *the rage* of travelling *is a symptom* of a deeper unsoundness affecting the whole intellectual action. *The intellect is vagabond,* and our *system* of education *fosters restlessness.*

Note the simple subject-predicates without connectives: *Travelling is a fool's paradise . . . I pack my trunk, embrace my friends . . . I seek the Vatican . . .* To these, what are the simplest additions? The modifying noun *fool's,* the adjectival *our first,* the phrases *to us* and *of places.* Then the patterned parallel additives, *at home, at Naples, at Rome;* and *on the sea, at Naples, beside me,* culminating in a pile-up of adjectives—*the stern fact, the sad self, unrelenting, identical.* Also then, the subordinate clauses, *the self that I fled from, but I am not, wherever I go,* are not very complicated, and, along with the phrases, less structurally important than the simple temporal sequence of verbs: *is, discover, dream, pack, embrace, wake up, seek, affect, go, fosters, travel, are forced.*

Notice that simple subject, predicate, and modification need no connectives: that connectives come in by adding place, time, manner, cause; that is, the phrasal and clausal specifications of simple modifiers. The proportioning of parts of speech is characteristic of Emerson's style—one adjective to three nouns, to two verbs to two connectives—and this proportion is characteristic also of what we may call the predicative or active verbal style, typified by such a sentence perhaps as: *The bright boy came to the beach and built a boat.* Alternative emphases would increase either the adjectival or phrasal modification, on the one hand, or clauses and clausal connectives on the other—both thus with richer modification, with assumption, rather than statement, of qualifying data.

Emerson's style puts a maximum premium, for English prose, on the separate items of predication, the free functioning of active verbs. Whitman differs; he substantiates with phrasal connectives: *in, into, of, with,* and the comparative or alternative *or* and *than;* with the barest minimum of causal and relative terms. His adjectives and nouns and connectives are more than Emerson's, his verbs less; he is one of the few for whom many verbs are given the form of adjective participles, three times as many as Emerson's. In the third paragraph of *Democratic Vistas,* Whitman in effect introduces his style as well as his subject:

> But preluding no longer, *let me strike the key-note* of the following strain. First premising that, though the passages of it have been written different times, (*it is,* in fact, *a collection* of memoranda, perhaps for future designers, comprehenders,) and though it may be open to the charge of one part contradicting another—for there are opposite sides to the great question of democracy, as to every great question—*I feel the parts* harmoniously blended in my own realization and convictions, *and present them* to be read only in such oneness, each page and each claim and assertion modified and temper'd by the others. *Bear in mind,* too, *that they are not the result* of studying up in political economy, but of the ordinary sense, observing, wandering among men, these States, these stirring years of war and peace.

Here no more than a fifth of the material is direct predicate of subject, in contrast to Emerson's half. Whitman admits the possible charge of self-contradiction, but dismisses conscious contradiction, so strong for Emerson, from his style—"each claim and assertion modified and tempered by the others." Modification is the key-note, and sensory modification, not from argument, but from observing, wandering. *In, into, of, with, or, than:*

> *Our fundamental want* today in the United States, with closest, amplest reference to present conditions, and to the future, *is* of a class, and the clear idea of a class, of native authors . . . accomplishing . . . a religious and moral character beneath the political and productive and intellectual bases of the States. . . . *Never was anything more wanted* than, today, and here in the States, the poet of the modern is wanted, or the great literatus of the modern.

Between these extremes of Whitman and Emerson, there is a middle ground—not a mere compromise, but a mode of its own, as its vocabulary exemplifies. Note Twain's chapters 15, 16, 17, in *Life on the Mississippi,* for example. The chief connectives are prepositional like Whitman's, but of a more directional adverbial sort; *about, at, between, on, through, to, under, upon;* with, like

Emerson, a minimum of locative and possessive terms. While Whitman's prepositions of place show presence or possession, Twain's show action, benefiting his stronger use of verbs:

> At the first glance, *one would suppose that* when it came to forbidding information about the river *these two parties could play equally* at that game; *but this was not so.* At every good-sized town from one end of the river to the other, *there was a "wharf-boat"* to land at, instead of a wharf or a pier. *Freight was stored* in it for transportation; waiting *passengers slept* in its cabins.

Here about a third of the material is direct predication of subject, between Emerson's half and Whitman's fifth, just as Twain's style in general balances adjectives and verbs.

. . .

Time, with its general lessening of connectives, limits in its way the choices of a writer today, making probable the shortening of his sentences to forty, rather than an older seventy, words, cutting down the probabilities of strong logical connective use, and raising the chances for the adverbials. Within time and type then, the individual writer makes his own unique combinations of choice.

What it seems to me important for the young writer to know is what these choices are, how they have been made in the past, and how he may make them in the present. They are not infinitely various, for example, but limited and significant for certain tones and attitudes: the phrasal, for a receptive objectivity of observation, as in many scientific writers; the balanced, for a reasoned subordination; the active verbal for a commitment to natural temporal sequence, events as they happen. What the writer chooses to say about his subject, and how he develops and composes it is a matter of his awareness of, his power over, his thought and language. To think of him as only individual robs him of his participation in values, makes him a mere atom among the rest. But he is not. As an artist he is most solidly a worker in the values of his medium. So the student is the young artist too. Once he is able to see how others have worked before him, how others work around him, and once he is able to estimate the powers of his own language, he can consider deliberately, weigh and reject consciously, plan and proceed effectively, with a sense that his fate is at least partially, in composition, in his own hands; that he can decide where he wants to go, and then go there.

From choices, let us turn to necessities: the

writer's commitments to predication. Suppose a student is considering the question, What does the first scene of *Hamlet* do for the play as a whole? And suppose he decides a good answer is: "The first scene establishes Hamlet in the view of his contemporaries, a view emphasized first by Horatio, then by Laertes, Rosencranz and Guildenstern, and Fortinbras." Then he knows first of all that his predicate is *establishes Hamlet* and that the steps of unfolding this predicate will be the steps of his paragraphs. The *first scene* is the subject; from it the material relevant to the predicate will be drawn. The predicate then is further modified by two phrases—*in the view,* and *of his contemporaries.* And finally, the last phrase of the question, *for the play as a whole,* is prepared to be dealt with in the apposition, *a view emphasized by Horatio, Laertes, and others.* In other words, both question and answer consider what possible predications can be made for Scene I, and then proceed to select and develop one of them. It is not the substance of Scene I which will guide the essay; rather, it is the pertinence which the predication will attribute to Scene I as its subject. In such a way, the writer is master of his material. He is not conditioned by his material, rather he is faithful to it in terms of the responsibility he takes toward it, and the evidence he finds and provides for the predication—in our instance, for the statement *establishes Hamlet*—and then for the views of Hamlet's companions throughout the play, even to the final speech of Fortinbras.

. . .

In the word *grammar,* as admirable as *composition,* lies a fairly simple, or simplifiable, answer to our questions. Grammar gives us the articulations of language with which we can compose. And they are not infinitely multiple and confusing; rather they are fairly basic and elemental: the individual and powerful purpose of the predicate; the relevant substance of the subject; the specifiable details of manner and location in modifying clause, phrase, and word, and the explicit formal guidance of connectives: thus we compose our purpose in substance, quality, order and linkage. To know our purpose is not easy; it takes a philosophy. To know the malleability of our medium is not easy; it takes an art. But difficulty need not mean confusion. The composer in language, young or old, can look at his language and see its potentialities for his purposes and for purposes beyond him. Grammar for him can be as clear, strong, and potentially expressive as for the most accomplished artist. Our own best principles of coherence, would we apply them to our language, would tell us that we need not lose sight of the forest for the innumerable small branches of the trees.

It is the grain of the living wood we are after, the character of the language by which we live and compose.

suggestions for discussion and writing

1. What specific features of the grammar of a sentence does Professor Miles feel are of most interest to a student of composition and style? What value, in her opinion, does the study of grammar have for the writer?

2. Are Professor Miles's views on the design of an essay similar to or different from those of Gorrell? Explain.

3. Do Professor Miles's emphases in the study of style seem to you similar to, or different from, those of Christensen? Explain.

4. Using Professor Miles's concepts, examine the style of a few paragraphs by any well-known twentieth-century writer, and then describe his style.

5. Using Professor Miles's concepts, analyze your own style, as exemplified in a recent theme, and then describe it as precisely as you can. Can you say what tone or attitude you regularly take toward a subject? Can you say whether this tone or attitude is well chosen? Having identified it, would you like to alter or vary it? How might you do so?

6. In light of *your* experience with writing up to this time, and in light of this essay, do *you* think that the study of grammar has value for one who wishes to learn to write well? Why or why not?

7. Read the essay, "Literature as Sentences," by Richard Ohmann (*College English,* January 1966, pp. 261–267). Do you think the emphases in Ohmann's analyses of passages from literature are similar to Professor Miles's emphases in the analyses that are part of this essay? Explain your judgment. Both Ohmann and Miles discuss "grammar." What does each mean by "grammar"? Does each have the same kind of "grammar" in mind? Defend your answer.